the MARTYRDOM REMEMBERED

the MARTYRDOM REMEMBERED

A one-hundred-fifty-year perspective on the assassination of Joseph Smith

ASPEN BOOKS/SALT LAKE CITY, UTAH 1994

Library of Congress Cataloging-in-Publication Data

Bitton, Davis, 1930–
    The martyrdom remembered : a 150-year perspective on the assassination of Joseph Smith /
by Davis Bitton.
    p. cm.
Includes bibliographical references and index.
    ISBN 1-56236-213-5 : $ 16.95
    1. Smith, Joseph, 1805–1844—Assassination. 2. Mormons—United States—Biography. 4.
Mormon Church—Presidents—Biography. 5. Mormons—Attitudes. I. Title.
BX8695.S6B47 1994
289.3'092—dc20
[B]   94-16102
                                                            CIP

5 4 3 2 1

"Interior of Carthage Jail" by C. C. A. Christensen and "Carthage Jail" by C. C. A. Christensen
©Courtesy Museum of Art, Brigham Young University. All rights reserved.
"Panic in the Room," "Spiritual Witnesses," "The Martyred," "Forces of Opposition," "An Act of
Defense" ©Gary Smith. Used by permission.
Illustrations on pages 2, 28, 40, 84, 96, 104, 106 © The Church of Jesus Christ of Latter-day
Saints. Used by permission. Other graphics courtesy of Museum of Church History and Art,
Harold B. Lee Library at Brigham Young University, Utah State Historical Society.

Designed by Raymond C. Morales
Printed in the United States of America

Dedicated to the memory of Ronald W. Bitton and Lola Davis Bitton,
goodly parents, faithful followers of the Prophet.

Contents

Preface

For almost as long as I can remember, I have been interested in Joseph Smith and reading everything ever written by him or about him. Or at least trying to—each year that self-imposed goal becomes more difficult to reach. I have given talks about him and have stopped counting the lessons I have taught about his life and teachings. All of this was done with no intention of making any original contribution to scholarship.

Then somehow I began presenting papers at conventions on different aspects of his public image. I wish to thank the Mormon History Association for providing a forum on several occasions. Two of the chapters below appeared in a different form, as a single article, in *The John Whitmer Historical Association Journal*.

Curtis Taylor and Stan Zenk had the insight to recognize that a small book on *The Martyrdom Remembered* was worth doing and that it would not detract from my somewhat longer forthcoming book on *Images of the Prophet Joseph Smith*. As a complementary pair, these may find themselves on the shelf together; readers who enjoy one should enjoy the other.

As always, I am grateful to JoAn, my eternal companion, whose soul delighteth in the scriptures.

Prologue

"The Prophet is dead!" With this anguished cry, one of the characters in the film *Legacy* announces the terrible event of 27 June 1844 to Latter-day Saints working at a stone quarry. Something like this must indeed have occurred, as in Nauvoo itself, in other settlements, and in every Latter-day Saint household the melancholy news was relayed.

The Mormons were hearing of the death by assassination of their leader, Joseph Smith, and his brother Hyrum, who had been murdered while prisoners at the jail in Carthage, Illinois. The details leading up to that fatal event are not the subject matter of this book. Nevertheless, certain high points need to be understood as a background to what follows.

Joseph Smith had faced opposition for much of his life. His description of a vision in 1820 had led to ridicule. His retrieval of gold plates, from which the Book of Mormon was translated, provoked a number of attempts to take them from him by force. When the church later to be designated The Church of Jesus Christ of Latter-day Saints was organized in 1830, groups unfriendly to Joseph Smith tore down the temporary dam that had provided a small pond for baptizing new converts.

When Smith and his followers moved to Ohio in 1831, they did not leave persecution behind. In the new location, as early as 1832, Joseph Smith and Sidney Rigdon were dragged from their homes at night, beaten, and tarred and feathered. Later, in 1837, the failure of a bank Smith and others had founded at Kirtland led to angry denunciations and threats. For his own safety he fled under the cover of night.

In the meantime, Missouri, named by Joseph Smith as the Zion of the last days, had been the setting for escalating violence against the Mormons, who had been driven from their homes in Jackson County into neighboring Clay, Daviess, and Caldwell counties. In *The Mormon Experience*, Leonard Arrington and I suggested that the following factors combined led to hatred of the Mormons in Missouri: fear of political influence, dislike of economic competition, and revulsion at a rival religion. As Mormonism was loathed and persecuted, so too was its leader, who became the symbol and focus of animosity.

No sooner did Joseph Smith arrive in Missouri than hostility broke out once again. A group of unfortunate Mormons, cowering behind the unchinked logs of an unfinished mill, were subjected to withering fire by mounted mobsters. The Mormon stronghold at Far West, a new city still under construction, was besieged. When Joseph Smith and other Mormon leaders emerged from the city under a flag of truce, wishing to parley with their armed opponents, they were seized. One general ordered that they be shot, but a courageous militia general, Alexander Doniphan, refused to carry out this illegal order. Instead, they were kept in chains and eventually thrown into a dungeon of the jail at Liberty, Missouri, there to remain for over five months.

During this time, the winter of 1838–39, Mormon refugees fled from Missouri to Illinois, where they were given protection. Escaping his captors, Joseph Smith joined his family along the banks of the Mississippi River in Illinois and proceeded to lay out a new city and gathering place known as Nauvoo (a Hebrew word meaning "the beautiful"). The city grew steadily during the next three or four years as refugees and converts arrived. But once again anti-Mormonism raised its vicious head. The Mormons were denounced, with special vilification directed against their prophet, Joseph Smith.

Why did Smith and the Mormons possess this disconcerting ability to arouse opposition? Why did many of their friends in Illinois turn into enemies? The basic cause was once again a powerful convergence of political, economic, and religious motivations; those who did not fear or hate them for one of these reasons might well do so for another. But in Illinois additional specific aggravations appeared.

One of these was Masonry. The establishment of a lodge at Nauvoo in 1842 can be considered as a bid for middle-class respect, an attempt to build a collegial bond for mutual political benefit, a possible influence on the development of Mormon temple ceremonies, or a continuation of earlier Masonic associations by some Mormons.[1] But the lodge also led to a rapid increase in the number of Mormon Masons, which ultimately roused apprehension and opposition of other Illinois Masons. This source of resentment could then readily combine with others.

Doctrinal developments at Nauvoo introduced beliefs that, similarly, would not endear Mormons to their neighbors. These included baptism for the dead, the temple endowment ceremony, eternal marriage, exaltation and potential divine status for humans, and plural marriage.[2] It was especially plural marriage—usually known as polygamy—that aroused hatred. The other beliefs could be dismissed as bizarre or ridiculous, but the taking of more than one wife was an affront to the inherited moral code of their neighbors. Even though the doctrine was not publicly announced and the few who participated in it were pledged to secrecy, disaffected members blew the whistle. Soon it became one of the charges made against the Mormons sure to provoke a horrified reaction.

The political results of such opposition were inescapable. Earlier in Ohio and Missouri, under the sting of persecution, Mormons

NAUVOO EXPOSITOR.

—THE TRUTH, THE WHOLE TRUTH, AND NOTHING BUT THE TRUTH.—

VOL. I.] NAUVOO, ILLINOIS, FRIDAY, JUNE 7, 1844. [NO. 1.

THE "NAUVOO EXPOSITOR"
Is published on Friday of each week, and furnished to subscribers on the following

TERMS:

PUBLISHERS.
WILLIAM LAW, WILSON LAW, CHARLES
IVINS, FRANCIS M. HIGBEE, CHAUNCEY L.
HIGBEE, ROBERT D. FOSTER, CHARLES A.
FOSTER.

POETRY.

THE LAST MAN.

BY THOMAS CAMPBELL.

All worldly shapes shall melt in gloom,
The sun himself shall die,
Before this mortal shall assume
Its immortality!
I saw a vision in my sleep,
That gave my spirit strength to sweep
Adown the gulf of time!
I saw the last of human mould,
That shall creation's death behold,
As Adam saw her prime!

[The remainder of the body text consists of a serialized story and the beginning of the "PREAMBLE," set in small type across multiple columns.]

PREAMBLE.

It is with the greatest solicitude for the salvation of the Human Family, and of our own souls, that we have this day assembled.

"The Truth, The Whole Truth, And Nothing But The Truth"—The Nauvoo Expositor, Friday, 7 June 1844.

voted as a bloc for candidates friendly to them, which caused
the opposing candidates to see them as a threat, or even as anti-
American. In Illinois, despite the Church's efforts to prevent it, the
same situation developed. In the spring of 1844, one of Joseph
Smith's motives for running for the United States presidency was to
avoid alignment of the Mormons with either of the major parties.
Whigs had opposed the Mormons already, and now Democrats had
reason to do so as well.

In a more general sense, as Marvin S. Hill has argued, the Mormon
church simply appeared to outsiders as a monolithic entity incompatible with American pluralism. In other words, even with religious
and political matters set aside, the Mormons were a growing, unified
group that just did not fit in. As they grew in number and their
beliefs appeared less and less mainstream, it became increasingly
easier for others to see the Mormons as a nuisance or a threat. And
at their head stood their leader, the cause of it all, Joseph Smith.

From the time Joseph Smith arrived in Illinois, he had to fear that
he would be returned to Missouri, where he had "escaped" from
Liberty Jail, to face trial. When the Mormons' arch-foe, Missouri
Governor Lilburn W. Boggs, was fired upon by an unknown assailant,
the Mormons were immediately suspected. Porter Rockwell, a friend
of the Prophet found in the vicinity of the attempted assassination,
was seized and imprisoned, and Joseph Smith was accused of being
an accessory-before-the-fact. Attempts were made to extradite him,
and once in 1843 marshals seized him and attempted unsuccessfully
to hurry him back to Missouri for trial.

With anti-Mormons in Illinois calling loudly for the suppression
of the Mormons and their expulsion from the state, a dissident
faction within the Church began denouncing the Prophet's claims to
authority and his practice of polygamy. When this faction published

an opposition newspaper, The *Nauvoo Expositor*, the Nauvoo city council met and authorized the mayor, Joseph Smith, to suppress it as a public nuisance. The *Expositor's* press was promptly destroyed, and the outcry was immediate: Joseph Smith had shown an intolerable disregard for the constitutional right of freedom of the press. Thomas Sharp, the anti-Mormon editor of the *Warsaw Signal,* urged that the answer to the latest outrage be made "with powder and ball." If the law could not provide an answer, then vigilantism must.

Such was the background that led to Joseph and Hyrum Smith's surrender to authorities, who took them to the county seat of Carthage and charged them with riot. Fearful for his safety, and with good reason, Joseph had earlier begun a flight to the West but returned when urged to do so by family and friends. Now, with the assurance of Illinois Governor Thomas Ford that he would be protected, Joseph, with Hyrum and a small group of friends, went to Carthage to face trial.

Joseph and Hyrum were charged with riot for the destruction of the *Expositor*, but the Mormons quickly posted the $500 bail. The prisoners might then have gone free except for the filing of a second charge, treason against the state for having declared martial law at Nauvoo. With no bail set for this capital crime, they were incarcerated on the second floor of the local jail.

The stage was set. On the afternoon of 27 June 1844, a mob converged on the jail, quickly dispersed the militia guards there (who were probably in cahoots with the mob), and stormed up the stairs. They forced their gun barrels through the door and fired, while others fired into the prisoners' window from the outside. In a few short minutes of scuffling, shouts, and shots the deed was done. Hyrum Smith was hit in the face and fell dead. With a revolver that had been smuggled in, Joseph attempted a futile defense. He got off

only three shots, wounding three members of the mob before he was
hit. After falling out the window to the ground below, he was
dispatched at point-blank range by the mobsters.

This was the murder of Joseph and Hyrum Smith. Not surprisingly,
the event was perceived differently by Mormons and non-Mormons.
The Latter-day Saints had lost the men they considered their
prophet and their patriarch. The mob felt they had rid the country
of a traitorous charlatan. But on all sides the martyrdom left in its
aftermath a world that struggled to explain, justify, condemn, or
somehow articulate the significance of what had happened under
darkening skies on that fateful day.

NOTES

1. Robert Bruce Flanders, *Nauvoo: Kingdom on the Mississippi* (Urbana: University
of Illinois Press, 1965), 247–49. The subject is explored at greater length in several
works by Mervin B. Hogan.

2. T. Edgar Lyon, "Doctrinal Development of the Church during the Nauvoo
Sojourn, 1839–1846," *Brigham Young University Studies* 15 (Summer 1975): 435–46.

The Aftermath:
Diaries and Letters

*Engraving of the jail at
Carthage, Illinois, by
Frederick Piercy.*

How did the Mormon people react when they heard of the violent death of their prophet? One truism about such losses is that they are beyond expression in words. Yet we are able to gain some glimpse into the emotional response of the Saints in these moments of trauma through the simple yet eloquent statements they made at the time in their diaries and letters.

The news spread quickly to Nauvoo then slowly made its way to the members in branches abroad and missionaries laboring in the field. The immediate reactions as expressed in the most natural, unaffected prose include stunned surprise and sentiments of aching grief and sorrow that seemed for a time too great to bear. Joseph had been their prophet, God's instrument to restore his gospel and church. He had been their general, their townsman, their friend, and with the sense of outrage, there followed an affirmation of the goodness, innocence, and greatness of the victims—and a mighty declaration that the restored gospel had not been defeated but would continue its triumphant march.

Warren Foote's journal entry of 28 June 1844 captures the shock of the Saints as the news reached Nauvoo:

Elihu Allen and I were working in the harvest field cutting his wheat when about three o'clock P.M. my wife came out and told us that word had just come that Joseph Smith and his brother Hirum was shot in Carthage Jail yesterday afternoon. I said at once, "that it cannot be so." Yet it so affected us that we dropped the cradle and rake and went home. We found that the word had come so straight that we could no longer doubt the truth of it. We all felt as though the powers of darkness had overcome, and that the Lord had forsaken His people. Our Prophet and Patriarch were gone!

with them Joseph endeavoured to escape by the window but was shot in his decent from without

William Richards who was also in the room escaped unhurt

The news of the assassination did not reach Nauvoo until the next morning In vain would it be for me to attempt to describe the feeling of consternation, dismay, and anguish that the sad intelligence produced

Never did man feel a greater sorrow for the loss of human friends than was felt for those two men

But they held their peace and said in their own hearts let God avenge the blood of his servants in his own due time and in his own way

On the 28th their bodies were brought in to Nauvoo for interment and were met by a large number of the inhabitants of the city about half a mile east of the Temple where they formed a procession and followed the corps's to the Mansion House of Joseph Smith (the procession being headed by the musicians who before their fife and muffled drum — there being a fifer in the border) by There they were addressed by W. W. Phelps and Willard Richards in a brief though very affecting manner upon the death of the Prophet and Patriarch and also in regard to our situation They advised the saints to be quiet and say but little and every man to mind his own business and let the Lord avenge the blood of his servants in his own way and in his own due time

In vain would it be for me to attempt to portray the conflicting feelings that prevailed in the breasts of the people at that time. To describe the sorrow

Pages from Benjamin F. Cummings's journal, telling of "The news of the assassination . . ."

Who now is to lead the Saints? In fact we mourned "as one mourneth for his only son." Yet after all the anguish of our hearts, and deep mourning of our souls a spirit seemed to whisper, "All is well. Zion shall yet arise and spread abroad upon the earth, and the kingdoms of this world shall become the Kingdom of our God and his Christ." So we felt to trust in God.[1]

Jacob Gibson similarly observed the "distress and many tears and weeping" found throughout Nauvoo in the days following the martyrdom. He notes that at a meeting in the public square, "the first murmurs, were revenge from almost every quarter." However, the speaker—probably Willard Richards—admonished the crowd to "'be still and know that God raineth, be composed and return to your homes.'" Later in the day, the bodies of the dead prophets were brought for viewing, but here Gibson's emotions overcame him. With unrefined eloquence he wrote: "but I cant describe the Sean no, no, no."[2]

Also at Nauvoo was Benjamin F. Cummings, who said, "In vain would it be for me to attempt to describe the feeling of consternation, dismay, and anguish that the sad intelligence produced. Never did man feel a greater sorrow for the loss of human friends that [than] was felt for these two men."[3] Aroet L. Hale, who later played the snare drums at the funeral ceremony, noted: "To See Stout men & Women Standing around in groops Crying & morning for the Loss of their Dear Prophet & Patriarch was Enough to break the hart of a Stone."[4] Sixteen-year-old John Lyman Smith, a cousin of the Prophet, said, "I could not weep for the fountain was dried up, for I would gladly have given my life for them, but so it was & it is not for me to judge for God Doeth all things well."[5]

Newel Knight, who had been a close friend of the Prophet since the beginning of the Church's history, attended the public viewing of the bodies on 29 June, the funeral services, and then the mock burial—the bodies would be buried later in secret to keep enemies from desecrating the graves.[6] He filled pages of his journal with his witness as to the character of both Joseph and Hyrum: "In the hour of prosperity they taught the people humility and meekness, in the hour of persecution they practised these virtues and no men have done a greater work on earth since the days of the Savior." But such language, however sincere, eventually proved too impersonal and Knight's feelings overflowed:

> O how I loved those men, and rejoiced under their teachings! it seems as if *all* is gone, and as if my very heart strings will break, and were it not for my beloved wife and dear children I feel as if I have nothing to live for, and would rejoice to be with them in the Courts of Glory. But I must live, and labor, and try to do good, and help to build up the kingdom of our God here on the earth. And I pray God my Father that I may be reconciled unto my lot, and live and die a faithful follower of the teachings of our *Murdered Prophet and Patriarch.*[7]

We are not far off, I think, in seeing this as a particularly eloquent statement of the feelings of all the Saints who both grieved and resolved to continue the work. Theirs was a grief tempered by faith: with their Prophet gone, the Saints looked to the God and gospel taught to them by Joseph for some measure of comfort.

Mail going out from the Saints in Nauvoo spread news of the martyrdom and captured the same sentiments. In a letter dated June 30, Vilate Kimball wrote to her "Dear Dear Companion," Heber C. Kimball, who was preaching in the East:

I saw the lifeless corpses of our beloved brethren when they were brought to their almost distracted families. Yea I witnessed their tears, and groans, which was enough to rend the heart of an adamant. Every brother and sister that witnessed the scene felt deeply to sympathyze with them. Yea, every heart is filled with sorrow, and the very streets of Nauvoo seem to mourn. Where it will end the Lord only knows.[8]

She went on to tell of an omen appropriate to Elizabethan tragedy. When the Nauvoo Legion was called out ten drums were found with blood on them. "No one could account for it," Vilate wrote. "They examined to see how many there was. They found ten, and while they were examining the eleventh there came a large drop on that." Vilate saw these as dismal omens of death. William Law had at one time taken Hyrum's place as Joseph's counsellor in the First Presidency, but had apostatized, been set up as prophet in his own church, and been involved in writs sworn out against Joseph at Carthage. He had now brought about the death of two through his traitorous actions and, Vilate concluded, would not be satisfied until nine more were murdered.

On July 18, less than a month after the event, Almira Mack, niece of Lucy Mack Smith, wrote to her sister, who had just lost a little son:

Your trouble, you think, is as much as you can bear; but it is not like Aunt Lucy's. What must have been her feelings at seeing two of her sons brought into the house dead? Murdered by wicked men. When your little boy was sick, you could be with him and administer to his wants, and when he was gone, you could bury him with decency. But this privilege she could not have. . . . These two of the noblest men on earth were slain, and for what? Was it for crimes they had committed? I answer NO, but it was because they professed the religion of Jesus Christ.

They were Prophets of the Lord, and they laid down their lives as did the Prophets in ancient days.[9]

It is uncertain how comforting this kind of comparison was, but there can be little doubt as to Almira's feelings and perceptions. The sense of outrage still burned strong. The deaths were cruel and undeserved; the righteous had been slain by the hands of the wicked. She closes with a testimony that elevates the Prophet and his brother to the status of martyrs.

The power of that moment, when news came to Nauvoo of the murders at Carthage, did not diminish over time for Lucy Walker Kimball, later a plural wife of Heber C. Kimball. Writing many years later, she vividly recalled her own shock at hearing the news, which at first seemed almost beyond belief:

At the ernest solicitation of Gen. Don Carlos Smith's widow, some prior to Prest. Smith's death, Prest. Smith consented to me making my home with her, and she was an elder sister to me. We had just retired on the night of 27th June, when there came a loud rap at the door below. News, I cried, and fled down stairs, opened the door. A messenger quietly said Joseph and Hyrum have been murdered. I seemed paralized with terror, had no power to speak or move. Agnes, called out what is the news, receiving no answer, came rushing down to learn the awful truth. When at length we returned to our chamber and on our bended knees poured out the anguish of our souls to that God who holds the destinies of his children in his own hands, for a time it seemed utterly impossible that he would allow his prophet to be slain by his foes. . . .

The Dogs howled and barked, the cattle bellowed and all

creation was astir. We kept by the open window with our arms around each other, untill the dawn, witnessing the terrible commotion and calling to mind his profetic words. My soul sikens as I recall the anguish of the whole people as they crowded around his lifeless body and that of his noble brother Hyrum who was so true to him.[10]

Harvey Harris Cluff was only about eight years old at the time of the martyrdom. However, a retrospective statement in his autobiographical journal records similar, if less detailed, feelings that again demonstrate the power memories of the martyrdom held over the minds of the Saints: "I shall never, no never! eradicate from my mind the crushed feeling that fell upon me."[11] John Loveless, returning from a preaching mission to Ohio, remembered being on a Mississippi river boat when the announcement of the murders was made. Incredibly, to Loveless, the crowd on board with him cheered. "Had I possessed the strength of Sampson," he wrote, "I would, like him, have sunk the whole mass in one gulf of oblivion and sent them to their congenial spirits, howling devils of the infernal regions."[12]

Many of the journal references, like John Loveless's, were recorded by people who were not in Nauvoo at the time of the tragedy. To help promote Joseph Smith's candidacy for the presidency of the United States, almost every available man, including all but three of the Apostles, had left on preaching tours and were widely scattered. News traveled slowly. The murder, which occurred on 27 June 1844, was not reliably reported in some places for a week or two or even longer.

Some of those who were away from Nauvoo later told of experiencing premonitions on 27 June, which they only later discovered to be the date of the awful event. Erastus Snow wrote in his *Autobiography*:

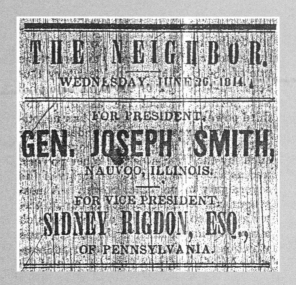

THE NEIGHBOR.

WEDNESDAY, JUNE 26, 1844.

FOR PRESIDENT,

GEN. JOSEPH SMITH,

NAUVOO, ILLINOIS.

FOR VICE PRESIDENT,

SIDNEY RIGDON, ESQ.,

OF PENNSYLVANIA.

One of many public
notices in support of
Joseph Smith's
candidacy for the presi-
dency of the United
States in 1844.

Although at that time I was ignorant of the awful tragedy which had occurred, I felt resting down upon me a more dreadful pressure of sorrow and grief and sense of mourning, than I had ever before felt, but knew not why.[13]

Parley P. Pratt recalled something similar. A day or two before the murder occurred he was "constrained by the Spirit to start prematurely for home." On a canal boat in New York state, with his brother William as traveling companion, he had an ominous experience:

> As we conversed together on the deck, a strange and solemn awe came over me, as if the powers of hell were let loose. I was so overwhelmed with sorrow I could hardly speak; and after pacing the deck for some time in silence, I turned to my brother William and exclaimed—"Brother William, this is a dark hour; the powers of darkness seem to triumph, and the spirit of murder is abroad in the land; and it controls the hearts of the American people, and a vast majority of them sanction the killing of the innocent. My brother, let us keep silence and not open our mouths."[14]

Pratt went on to state that, according to his calculations, "it was the same hour that the Carthage mob were shedding the blood of Joseph and Hyrum Smith, and John Taylor, near one thousand miles distant."

On 6 July John D. Lee, then preaching in Kentucky, first heard rumors of the murder. That night, as explained in his journal, he received angelic confirmation of the Prophet's death when a heavenly messenger uttered these words: "Instead of electing your leader the chief magistrate of the Nation—they have Martyrd him in prison—which has hasten[ed] his exaltation to the exutive chair over this generation." When the additional confirmation of a letter from Nauvoo was received, Lee gave vent to his feelings: "The feeling of grief and anguish operated so powerful upon my natural effections as to destroy the strength of mind & rendered it almost impossible for me to fill my appointments."[15]

Orson Hyde referred to such experiences in his own account of "that awful night" of 27 June. This was a night, Hyde asserts, when "there was an unspeakable something, a portentous significancy in the firmament" and "multitudes felt the whisperings of woe and grief." Hundreds of miles from the scene of the crime, he says, two unnamed apostles became "unaccountably sad" and filled with "unspeakable anguish of heart." He also mentions a president of the high priests who, while in Kentucky, had a vision of the bodies of the two martyrs.[16]

Just how much of this was truly noted on the night of June 27 and how much of it is refracted through the lens of later reflection? We will probably never know for sure, but it seems likely that two of the themes already noticed—(1) the awareness of people far from the event that something was wrong and (2) the vivid picture of howling dogs and disturbed cattle, with "all creation" astir—were heightened after the fact. Whatever feelings people had—or remembered having—on that night, it was easy to project back onto them an extraordinary significance.

What we can say is that such description combined with interpretation became common. In the "documentary history" of the Church there is an insertion by the Church historians of the mid-nineteenth century that credits the following with "depression" or sadness on the "memorable day" of 27 June: Brigham Young, Wilford Woodruff, Heber C. Kimball, Orson Hyde, Parley P. Pratt, George A. Smith, and Amasa Lyman.[17]

James Holt, preaching in Lebanon, Tennessee, on 27 June, was just concluding his sermon before a large congregation when "the spirit of revelation" came upon him. He told the crowd "that the enemies of the Church had taken the Prophet of God [that] day and put him to death, as they had all the prophets of God in all dispensations of the world." "'Now,'" he told his audience, "'you may have this for a testimony of the Gospel, for that is true Mormonism.'" He looked out the window at the setting sun. He offered to answer any questions, but there were none. "All seemed struck with amazement, and their eyes were full of tears." The next day, when he told his father about Joseph Smith's death, his father was skeptical. "He said he did not believe anyone could know anything for a certainty at such a distance. I told him that the spirit of God could reveal anything to man that was going on in any part of the world, and I knew that God had revealed the truth to me, and that I should start for home right away." Even Holt's missionary companion, Jackson Smith, could not believe this.[18]

This account was written thirty-seven years after the fact, and again is probably somewhat embellished, although description of the exact setting and the names of those who in principle might be able to confirm this testimony lend it some credence.

We must remember, too, that for many months threats and efforts to take Joseph Smith back to Missouri for trial had been hanging over the Prophet's head, and by 1844 anti-Mormons in Illinois were threatening to use whatever force was necessary to rid themselves of the Mormons and their leaders. The possibility of violent attacks and murders had to be in the minds of many Mormons; we know that Joseph Smith himself was preoccupied with such thoughts. It does not stretch credibility to think that some Mormons were brooding about such things at about the time the assassinations occurred, but actual dreams or visions informing people of the martyrdom appear to have been rare.[19]

In Massachusetts Wilford Woodruff had been hearing rumors of the Prophet's death for several days. On 9 July he found a detailed report of the martyrdom in the Boston *Times* and recorded it in his journal with this comment: "My prayer is that God will prepare our minds for the worst & that we may maintain our integrity untill death, that we may overcome as Jesus has overcome."[20]

The news from Nauvoo was fragmentary. Woodruff wrote, "We do not obtain one word from any of our friends so that we can obtain any thing correct upon the subject. I hope we may get something soon." He noted the mob spirit in the country and the outbreak of war between Texas and Mexico, concluding that "the world is sheding the blood of prophets Patriarch & Saints in order to fill up their cup."

On 17 July Brigham Young arrived in Boston. He and Woodruff walked to 57 Temple Street, the home of a Church member, where they could have some privacy. By this time, Woodruff knew that the Prophet was dead, and here he gave himself over to his feelings of sorrow:

> I have never shed a tear since I heard of the death of the prophet untill this morning but my whole soul has felt nerved up like steel.
>
> Br Young took the bed and I the big Chair, and I here veiled my face and for the first time gave vent to my grief and mourning for the Prophet and Patriarch of the Church Joseph and Hiram Smith who were murdered by a gentile mob. After being bathed in a flood of tears I felt composed.

Heber C. Kimball first heard the news on 9 July, when he recorded the following:

The papers were full of News of the death of our Prophet. I was not willen to believe it, for it was to much to bare. the first news I got of his death was on Tuesday morning . . . it struck me at the heart.[21]

The next few days were days of uncertainty. Elder Kimball went on to Baltimore with delegates, apparently still planning to hold a nominating convention for Joseph Smith. On 12 July he and Lyman Wight picked up mail that told them of events in Nauvoo up to 19 June, at which time the Prophet was still alive and free. Kimball and Wight prayed fervently "that we might get some definite news." In the evening they picked up a letter that told of events up to 24 June, when Joseph and Hyrum were incarcerated in Carthage Jail. "This letter satisfied us that the Brethren ware dead O Lord what feelings we had."

On Sunday, 14 July, Kimball broke the news to a congregation of Saints in Philadelphia. He reported, "great sorrow prevailed and agreed to dress in morning. O Lord How can we part with our dear Br, O Lord save the Twelve." The next day he left for New York and from there went on to Boston, arriving on 18 July. There he found Brigham Young, Orson Hyde, Orson Pratt, and Wilford Woodruff, all of whom, as Kimball noted, "felt Sorrifull for the Loss of our Prophet and Patriarch."

Preaching in Canada and upper New York was Alfred Cordon, who heard of the event on 9 July, but "did not credit the statement as we had heard of their death so many times." Not until 26 July did Cordon and his missionary companion read a newspaper account that convinced them: "we returned to Mr. Parkhurst's very sorrowfull, we did not fully credit the report till now."[22]

James Madison Fisher, not quite a teenager at the time, remarked that "everything seemed black as ink."[23] William Hyde said, "My soul sickened and I wept before the Lord and for a time it seemed that the very Heavens were clad in mourning."[24] In Pennsylvania, William I. Appleby noted in his diary on 10 July: "Heard of the murder of Br. Joseph & Hyrum Smith by a Mob at Carthage, Illinois. Staid over night at Br. S. Bringhursts. I could not credit the Report of their deaths at first, indeed I did not want to believe it, and almost hoped against hope!"[25]

More than a month after the assassinations, on August 11, Brigham Young was still moved by accounts of how the news had been received in Nauvoo. Writing to his daughter Vilate, he said, "It has ben a time of morning. The day that Joseph and Hyrum ware braught from Cartheg to Nauvoo it was judged by manny boath in and out of the church that there was more than 5 barels of tears shead. I cannot bare to think enny thing about it."[26]

Jane James, a young black woman who was employed as a servant in the Smith household, gave her testimony many years later, but it is entirely consistent with what Brigham Young and others said in late June and July of 1844: "When he was killed, I liked to a died myself, if it had not been for the teachers, I felt so bad. I could have died, jus laid down and died; and I was sick abed, and the teachers told me, 'You don't want to die because he did. He died for us, and now we all want to live and do all the good we can.'"[27]

The news eventually reached Church members in other parts of the world. One of the last to hear of the martyrdom was Benjamin F. Grouard, who was preaching Mormonism in the Society Islands. After taking passage on a ship to Tahiti on 1 February 1845, he found the newspapers telling of the event. He found the account "so contradictory & improbable that I did not know what to believe," but remembered a dream in which he had seen the bodies of Joseph and

Hyrum. Not until 25 February 1845 did Grouard receive reliable news, which led to the following journal entry:

> Tuesday Feb 25th the sad news came fully confirmed. The whale ship Averic had been cast away on Raitea, an Island one hundred miles to the leaward, & consiquenty her papers &c came to Tahiti & among the rest was the governors letter addressed to the citizens of Illinois stating the particulars of the assasination of "Joseph & Hyrum Smith." Though we had been looking for & partialy expecting such news from the many flying reports which had already come, yet when we were thus fully convinced of its truth it was a dreadful shock to us—one which we were illy prepared to receive. The heartrending anguish it caused us I will not attempt to discribe—: that our beloved prophet & patriarch were gone—gone to return no more—to rejoyce—that we must return to the church & find their places vacant who had blessed us in the name of the Lord & told us to go in peace & prosper, those who held the cause of Zion so close to their hearts, who lived for it, laboured for it, & died for it—that we could see them no more, no more hear their voices till we meet them in the celestial kingdom of God it was bitter, bitter, more than words can tell.[28]

He went on to express his indignation toward the murderers, the state of Illinois, and even the United States, concluding, "you have accomplished what you have sought for these last 14 years, & now look out for the judgements of God."

That the judgments of God included apocalyptic events, that the Prophet's death, in other words, was but one scene in the great drama of the Last Days, was suggested by more than one Latter-day Saint. On 24 July 1844 the *Nauvoo Neighbor* reported not only on the martyrdom but also on the latest outbreak of mob violence in

Philadelphia. The *Neighbor* then editorialized: "O Liberty where hast thou fled? Has the Lamb opened the second seal, spoke of by John the Revelator, and given the rider on the red horse the great sword, and power to take peace from the earth."[29]

Lucy Walker Kimball, in her account of the night in which she heard the news, records that after the shock she and Agnes Smith wondered why God would allow such a thing to happen:

> Why not? His only begotten Son offered his life as a sacrifice. What did Joseph say when he gave himself up, at the solicitation of those who plead he would not forsake his flock, "If my life is worth nothing to you it is worth nothing to me." He well knew what his destiny was when he gave up the plan of flying to the "Rocky Mountains." How we plead that Father would, as he had done fifty times before, save him from his foes. But he gave his life cheerfully to save the people. He had often said he would not die a natural death but by the hands of his enemies. That he made every preparation for this great sacrifice we well knew, as we called to mind his own words and yet felt unprepared for the blow, when it came. . . . We kept by the open window with our arms around each other, untill the dawn, witnessing the terrible commotion and calling to mind his profetic words.[30]

Again, this valuable account, full of detail, combines the real experience with the later reintegrating and reflection that probably could not have been accomplished the very night of the martyrdom.

There is no reason to doubt the shock and grief felt by the Saints. It is clear, too, that they instinctively sought an explanation that would leave their faith intact. Several of the early statements point to what the story of the martyrdom would become: a mighty testimony to the character and mission of the Prophet and martyr of the Restoration.

NOTES

1. Warren Foote Journal, 28 June 1844, LDS Church Archives. Descriptions and synopses of unpublished diaries and journals cited here can be found in my *Guide to Mormon Diaries and Autobiographies* (Provo, Utah: Brigham Young University Press, 1977).

2. Jacob Gibson Journal, LDS Church Archives. When exact dates are not given, the relevant passages can readily be found in the entries for late June or early July 1844.

3. Benjamin Franklin Cummings Journal, Harold B. Lee Library, Brigham Young University, Provo, Utah.

4. Aroet Lucius Hale Journal, LDS Church Archives.

5. John Lyman Smith Journal, LDS Church Archives.

6. After the bodies had been laid out for public viewing, they were hidden in the Mansion House while sand and gravel were placed inside the coffins. These two coffins were then placed inside plainer ones, nailed shut, and buried in a cave near the Nauvoo Temple. The primary fear was that someone would secretly dig up the bodies and take them to Missouri, where a reward had been offered for the return of Joseph Smith, dead or alive. See Barbara Hands Bernauer, "Still 'Side by Side'—The Final Burial of Joseph and Hyrum Smith," *John Whitmer Historical association Journal* 11 (1991): 17–33.

7. William G. Hartley, *"They Are My Friends": A History of the Joseph Knight Family, 1825–1850* (Provo, Utah: Grandin Book Co., 1986), 152–54.

8. Vilate Kimball, letter to Heber C. Kimball, 30 June 1844, in Stanley B. Kimball, *Heber C. Kimball, Mormon Patriarch and Pioneer* (Urbana: University of Illinois Press, 1981), 108.

9. Almira Mack Covey, letter to Temperance Mack, 18 July 1844, in John C. Cumming, *The Pilgrimage of Temperance Mack* (Mount Pleasant, Mich.: privately printed, 1967), 41–47.

10. Lucy Walker Kimball, letter in LDS Church Archives. A plural wife of Joseph

Smith, Lucy was widowed by the martyrdom. Her marriage to Heber C. Kimball took place on 8 February 1845, her sealing to Kimball for time on 15 January 1846. See Stanley B. Kimball, *Heber C. Kimball,* 314.

11. H. H. Cluff Journal as quoted in Davis Bitton, *Guide to Mormon Diaries and Autobiographies* (Provo, Utah: Brigham Young University Press, 1977), 71.

12. John Loveless autobiography as reprinted in *Our Pioneer Heritage* 12 (1969): 221–26.

13. *Utah Genealogical and Historical Magazine* 14 (1923): 110.

14. Parley P. Pratt, *Autobiography* (New York: Russell Brothers, 1874), 331–34.

15. John D. Lee Diary, 6 July 1844, LDS Church Archives.

16. Joseph Smith, *History of the Church of Jesus Christ of Latter-day Saints* 7 vols. (Salt Lake City: Deseret News Press, 1902–1932), 7:132. I am following the traditional attribution. When the account first appeared in the *Millennial Star,* it was unsigned except for "Ed." The editor of the *Millennial Star* at the time was Orson Spencer. When it appeared later in *The Frontier Guardian,* again there was no byline. When it was published later in the *Elders' Journal,* it appeared under the byline of Orson Hyde.

17. Smith, *History of the Church,* 7:132–33.

18. "The Reminiscences of James Holt: A Narrative of the Emmett Company," *Utah Historical Quarterly* 23 (1955): 19–20.

19. After noting the lack of contemporary diary evidence, Dale L. Morgan writes: "It would seem that memories were afterwards distorted by the emotional need for personal participation in an overwhelming tragedy." "Reminiscences of James Holt," 20n.

20. Wilford Woodruff Journal, 17 July 1844, LDS Church Archives; published in Scott G. Kenney, ed., *Wilford Woodruff's Journal* 9 vols (Midvale, Utah: Signature Books, 1983).

21. Heber C. Kimball Journal, 9 July 1844, LDS Church Archives; published in Stanley B. Kimball, ed., *On the Potter's Wheel: The Diaries of Heber C. Kimball* (Salt Lake City: Signature Books, 1987).

22. Alfred Cordon Journal, LDS Church Archives.

23. James Madison Fisher Journal, LDS Church Archives.

24. William Hyde Journal, LDS Church Archives.

25. William I. Appleby Journal, LDS Church Archives, 10 July 1844.

26. Brigham Young, letter to Vilate Young, 11 August 1844, LDS Church Archives.

27. *Young Woman's Journal* 16 (1905): 553.

28. Benjamin F. Grouard Journal, microfilm, LDS Church Archives.

29. The same issue contained a report on "Millerism." Miller's prophecies of the Second Coming had not come to pass, but he had now recalculated. The Mormon newspaper ridicules Miller, refrains from being too specific about dates, and yet is still willing to see the riots and assassinations in the context of apocalypse.

30. Lucy Walker Kimball, letter in LDS Church Archives.

The Aftermath:
Poetry

2

נקים דם עבדך השפוך

LAMENTATION

Of a Jew among the afflicted and mourning Sons and Daughters of Zion, at the assassination of the Two Chieftains in Israel,

JOSEPH AND HYRUM SMITH.

Blessed the people knowing the shout of Jehovah,
In the light of his countenance they will walk.
How can we, a people in sackcloth,
Open our lips before thee?
They have rejected and slain our leaders,
Thine anointed ones.
Our eyes are dim, our hearts heavy;
No place of refuge being left.
Redeem the people that in thee only trusts:
There is none to stand between and inquire:
Thou art our helper,
The refuge of Israel in time of trouble.—
O look in righteousness upon thy faithful servants,
Who have laid bare their lives unto death,
Not withholding their bodies:
Being betrayed by false brethren, and their lives cut off,
Forbiding their will before thine:
Having sanctified thy great name,
Never polluting it;
Ready for a sacrifice;—standing in the breach,
Tried, proved and found perfect.
To save the blood of the fathers;
Their children, brothers, and sisters;
Adding theirs unto those who are gone before them;
Sanctifying thy holy and great name upon the earth:
Cover and conceal not their blood.
Give ear unto their cries until thou lookest

And shewest down from heaven—taking vengeance
And avenging their blood—avenging thy people and thy law,
According to thy promises made
Unto our forefathers, Abraham, Isaac, and Jacob.
Hasten the acceptable and redeeming year:
SHADDAY: remember unto us thy covenant:
All this heaviness has reached us:
Can any one be formed to declare
What has befallen us?
All this we bear, and the name of our God
We will not forget, nor deny,
The "Hebrews" God he is called,
Thou art clothed with righteousness,
But we are vile.
Come not in judgment with us.
Before thee nothing living is justified by their works.
But be with us as thou wast with our fathers.
Help thou, O Father; unto thee
We will lift our souls,
Our hearts in our hands,
We look to heaven,
Lifting our eyes unto the mountains,
From whence cometh our help.
Turn away thine anger,
That we be not spoiled.
O return and leave a blessing behind thee.

The anonymous Jew's "Lamentation" following the martyrdom, published on 15 July 1844.

Poetry about the martyrdom began appearing almost immediately. It included Eliza R. Snow's "The Assassination of Gen'ls Joseph Smith and Hyrum Smith," published in *Times and Seasons* on 1 July 1844, just four days after the event; the anonymous "Lamentation of a Jew among the Afflicted and Mourning Sons and Daughters of Zion, at the Assassination of the Two Chieftains in Israel," apparently penned by Alexander Neibaur and published on 15 July; and W. W. Phelps's "Praise to the Man," which appeared on 1 August.

In the aftermath of the martyrdom, Mormon poets struggled to convey their grief and sense of loss, especially that of the entire community. Among the poems, only William Hyde's "On the Death of Joseph and Hyrum Smith" and William Appleby's "Lines Suggested by the Reflections of the Calls and Martyrdom of the Prophet and Patriarch," neither of which was published, attempt to convey their personal reaction. Hyde, who was preaching the gospel in Vermont in June 1844, heard the news from a stranger.

> I listened to this stranger's tale
> Until my strength did almost fail;
> My blood did chill within my vein,
> From weeping I could not refrain.[1]

The more general grief of the Saints was conveyed by the anonymous Jew in his "Lamentation," a poetic prayer to God:

> How can we, a people in sackcloth,
> Open our lips before thee?
>
> . . . .
>
> Our eyes are dim, our hearts heavy;
> No place of refuge being left.[2]

And Charles Rogers, addressing Joseph Smith in his "On the Death of the Prophet," wrote:

> We feel thy loss, yea, tears of sadness
> Fill every eye in Zion's land;
> We would have met thy fate with gladness,
> Could we have staid thy murderers hand.[3]

As the poems move beyond factual descriptions of expressions of grief, they become especially effective. Consider, for example, the poets' feelings on the despicableness of the assassins. Eliza R. Snow sees the dead martyrs as a sacrifice "T'appease the ragings of a brutish clan,/ That has defied the laws of God and man!"[4] Sylvester Hulet's "O Earth Attend" calls on the Saints to "weep o'er the deeds just done by wicked hands."[5] William Hyde describes the Carthage mob as

> Those hellish fiends, in hellish form,
> Out from their coverts they did swarm.[6]

In Nelson W. Whipple's unpublished "The Two Martyrs," the assassins are "mobers vile . . . feindish men/ Who left them bleeding on the plain."[7]

If the assassins were fiendish, the crime was no less so. Sally Randall, a resident of Nauvoo, described the Martyrdom in a letter as "one of the most horrible crimes that ever history records. . . . Never has thare been such a horrible crime committed since the day Christ was crucified."[8] The poets agreed. In Eliza R. Snow's words, the mob's crime was "[t]he blackest deed that men or devils know / Since Calv'ry's scene."[9] For Sylvester Hulet

> ne er transpir'd on earth, (nor yet in hell)
> A scene more tragic since the Savior fell.[10]

This was not the death of two ordinary men, nor was it an ordinary murder—if there is such a thing. The prophet chosen to restore Christ's church and of whom Christ had said "his word ye shall receive, as if from mine own mouth" had been slain by the hands of murderers and apostates.[11] The martyrdom had cosmic importance, and the Saints grappled with words as they tried to express how important, how tragic, the event really was.

In the tradition of eulogy the Mormon writers wanted to say something about the character of the departed leaders. The murder was indeed a heinous crime, committed by diabolical men, and the horror was compounded by the saintly nature of the victims. John Taylor cries out in "O Give Me Back My Prophet Dear," printed a year after the murders at Carthage:

> O give me back my Prophet dear,
>   And Patriarch, O give them back;
> The Saints of latter days to cheer,
>   And lead them in the gospel track.
> But ah! they're gone from my embrace,
>   From earthly scenes their spirits fled;
> These two, the best of Adam's race,
>   Now lie entombed among the dead.[12]

According to "The Seer," also written by Taylor, Joseph was "of noble seed—of heavenly birth," and "His equal now cannot be found / By searching the wide world around."[13] Eliza R. Snow put it this way in "The Assassination":

> For never, since the Son of God was slain
> Has blood so noble, flow'd from human vein
> As that which now, on God for vengeance calls
> From "freedom's ground"—from Carthage prison walls!

Sampler by Mary Ann Broomhead with a verse commemorating the martyrdom stitched with her own hair.

Not only were the martyrs great and noble, but they were also innocent, and some writers were anxious to stress this point. Sylvester Hulet insists it was "righteous blood that now stains this guilty land." In "O Give Me Back My Prophet Dear," John Taylor pleads:

> Ye men of wisdom tell me why,
>> When guilt nor crime in them were found,
> Why now their blood doth loudly cry,
>> From prison walls, and Carthage ground.

Eliza R. Snow expressed the same idea in "The Assassination":

> Once lov'd America! what can atone
> For the pure blood of innocence, thou'st sown?
>
> . . . .
>
> Yes, blameless men, defam'd by hellish lies
> Have thus been offer'd as a sacrifice. . . .

Such protestations of blamelessness and innocence were surely in part Mormon reaction to Thomas Sharp and the anti-Mormon press, who had loudly denounced Joseph and Hyrum as criminals.[14] But it is hard to overlook the closeness of such an idea to that of the sacrificial lamb without spot or blemish—a type of the sacrifice of the sinless Son of God, Jesus Christ.

Like Christ's, the martyrs' sacrifice required the spilling of their *blood*, and blood becomes a powerful symbol for the lives and sacrifice of the martyrs in these poems. It was *innocent* blood that would stain Illinois (or that would plead unto heaven) and call upon God for vengeance. In her poem dated 1 July 1844, Eliza R. Snow tells how the murdered brothers had "seal'd their testimony with their blood." (Interestingly, on the very same day, 1 July, Sally Randall was writing a letter with the same idea expressed in prose: "The earth is deprived of the two best men there was on it. They have sealed thare testimony with thare blood."[15]) John Taylor's great tribute (now Section 135 in the LDS Doctrine and Covenants) stated that Joseph Smith, "like most of the Lord's anointed in ancient times, has sealed his mission and his works with his own blood; and so has his brother Hyrum." Somehow, the shedding of this blood, so often required of a prophet, serves as an irrefutable final testament to that prophet's mission.

In the poetry, the martyrs' sacrifice is also made by choice: With full knowledge of their impending fate, the brothers voluntarily return to give their lives. As the Jewish "Lamentation" put it:

> O look in righteousness upon thy faithful servants,
> Who have laid bare their lives unto death,
> Not withholding their bodies:
> Being betrayed by false brethren and their lives cut off,
> Forbiding their will before thine:
> Having sanctified thy great name,
> Never polluting it;
>
> Ready for a sacrifice;—standing in the breach,
> Tried, proved and found perfect.
> To save the blood of the fathers;
> Their children, brothers, and sisters.

John Taylor, in "The Seer," wrote of the Prophet Joseph:

> The saints;—the saints; his only pride,
> For them he liv'd, for them he died![16]

Joseph's own words about his sacrifice have been canonized to be held in remembrance by the Saints through the ages: "I am going like a lamb to the slaughter; but I am calm as a summer's morning; . . . I shall die innocent, and it shall be said of me—He was murdered in cold blood."[17]

It is evident that the martyrdom literature was attempting several things. It was an expression of grief, both in prose and poetry. It was an effort to condemn the assassins and deplore the shame of the country that had allowed such a thing to occur. It was an effort to proclaim in ringing words the greatness, the nobility, and the innocence of the martyrs, who had sealed their testimony with their blood and whose work would continue in the courts on high while the Church would continue its onward course below. But in particular, the authors sought to state in words the significance of the mission of Joseph Smith. What had he done that was so great? What was his real contribution that deserved such memorials? It went far beyond being innocent or noble or even dying for his cause and his people. We find in most of the martyrdom poems succinct statements of just how profound and far-reaching were the works of this prophet of God. Eliza R. Snow proclaims in "The Assassination":

> Oh wretched murd'rers! fierce for human blood!
> You've slain the prophets of the living God,
> Who've borne oppression from their early youth,
> To plant on earth, the principles of truth.
>
> . . . .
>
> We mourn thy Prophet, from whose lips have flow'd
> The words of life, thy spirit has bestow'd—
> A depth of thought, no human art could reach
> From time to time, roll'd in sublimest speech,
> From the celestial fountain, through his mind,
> To purify and elevate mankind:

> The rich intelligence by him brought forth,
> Is like the sun-beam, spreading o'er the earth.

In "Praise to the Man," by W. W. Phelps, Joseph was he who was anointed by Jesus, who communed with Jehovah, and who opened the last dispensation.[18] For John Taylor, Joseph the Seer was described as follows:

> With Gods he soared, in the realms of day;
> And men he taught the heavenly way.
>
> . . . .
>
> The chosen of God, and the friend of men,
> He brought the priesthood back again,
> He gazed on the past, on the present too;—
> And ope'd the heav'nly world to view.[19]

Such efforts to capture in poetic form the greatness and significance of Joseph Smith's mission did not end in 1844–45. Three years after the event, William I. Appleby brought together several of the themes as follows:

> Joseph, the Prophet of the Lord,—thy name to me is dear,—
> And to thy mem'ry now, I often drop the tender tear;
> Call'd thou wast, when young, thy faithfulness to prove,
> To do the work agreed by thee e'er thou left the courts above.
>
> On this terrestrial ball thou came, at the appointed time,
> To do those works of might and power, and let thy wisdom shine.
> To break the spell of darkness—the time had arriv'n
> To bring to light the truth, the way and plan of heav'n.

Appleby lists the signal achievements of his prophetic hero, starting with the Book of Mormon. Then:

Again the Priesthood is restor'd the Church is organized,
According to Revelation but by the world, despis'd—.

Built on the ancient pattern, (a dispensation new)
Of "Apostles, and Prophets," and inspiration too.—

The poem goes on to list the appearances of John the Baptist, Peter,
James, John, Elias, Elijah, and Moses. As for Smith's present role,
here is Appleby's conception:

Thou'st only pass'd behind the veil, to plead the cause above,
Of Mourning, bleeding Zion, which was thy daily love.—

As he builds to his crescendo, Appleby has no doubt of Joseph
Smith's continuing prophetic calling:

Thou art the "Angel of the Church" under Christ thy head—
Thou has minister'd to it since thy death,
    by thy counsels it is led.—

Thou wilt stand in thy place and lot, in the Resurrection morn,
With all the ancient worthies, whose brows a crown adorns—.
At the head of thy dispensation thou ever thus will stand,
While less inferior spirits,—shall bow at thy command.[20]

Though it is not great literature, Appleby's themes and sentiments
are common to those who tried to honor and capture the greatness
of their prophet in verse.

Of all the themes found in the poetry, most immediate to the
needs of the Saints in the days, weeks, and months following the
event was the question of what they should do. The poetry, which
might well have fanned the flames of anger, instead counseled
patience while at the same time calling for divine retribution or

vengeance. In "The Assassination of Gen'ls Joseph Smith and Hyrum Smith," Eliza R. Snow admonished: "Ye Saints! be still and know that God is just." In Parley P. Pratt's "Cry of the Martyrs," the victims themselves petition the Lord in a way that hearkens back to Joseph's cry to the Lord in Doctrine and Covenants section 121:

> "How long, O Lord! holy and true, dost thou
> Not judge and avenge our blood on them that
> Dwell on the earth?"
> The Lord, in turn, replies:
> BE PATIENT—O ye martyred souls and wait. . . .[21]

One Mormon woman close to the event, Sarah Griffith Richards, found that the poetic words that came to her again and again were those of John Milton in "On the Late Massacre in Piedmont":

> Avenge, O Lord, thy slaughtered saints, whose bones
> Lie scattered on the Alpine mountains cold,
> Even them who kept thy truth so pure of old
> When all our fathers worshiped stock and stones.[22]

If we compare any of the Mormon poetry with, say, the moving tribute to Abraham Lincoln "When Lilacs Last in Dooryard Bloom'd," it is apparent that the Mormons had no Walt Whitman. Powerful religious faith does not in itself assure great art. But the sincerity of the Saints' emotion is unquestionable. Nor is the truth of the religious claims at issue. The Mormon martyrdom poetry may be deficient in tone and concreteness, uninteresting in rhythm and rhyme, by academically critical standards, but it represented, in Wordsworth's phrase, the spontaneous overflow of human emotions deeply moved.

Perhaps in the interest of fairness, the basis of comparison should be shifted. Of the thousands, most likely millions, of poems written to pay tribute to departed loved ones, not many are truly memorable. At the deaths of Abraham Lincoln and John F. Kennedy, great quantities of verse were penned, some tasteful and eloquent but much of it mediocre. In these instances the poetic outpouring, good or bad, helped to express and to convey feeling and meaning; it represented, in addition, catharsis for the emotions of the survivors.

The Mormon martyrdom poetry did this too. More important, it succeeded in expressing in pieces that could be easily read, recited, and sung the basic ideas that helped to place the tragedy in earthly and eternal perspective. If the diaries and letters were unsurpassed as an account of the individual reactions to the sad news, the poetry did something more in its expression not only of grief but of *meaning*. It denounced the assassins; placed the dead leaders in the company of such venerable martyrs as Stephen, Peter, and Paul; explained how their testimony gained in force by their death; and went on to portray the comforting picture of the Prophet and Patriarch in the councils on high. A literature that does this does not necessarily achieve greatness, but it does accomplish some very important things for a community of believers, defining not only their loss, but themselves.

NOTES

1. William Hyde Journal, holograph, LDS Church Archives.
2. *Times and Seasons*, 15 July 1844, p. 591. Alexander Neibaur was a Jewish convert, born in Germany, who joined the Church in England. He lived in Nauvoo from 1841 to 1846 and later moved to Utah with the Saints. His diary entry of a conversation with Joseph Smith is one of the early accounts of the First Vision. A direct descendant of Alexander Neibaur states unequivocally that he authored the "Lamentation." See Theda Lucille Bassett, *Grandpa Was a Pioneer* (Salt Lake City: privately published, 1988), 26–27.

3. *The Prophet*, 10 August 1844.

4. "The Assassination of Gen'ls Joseph Smith and Hyrum Smith," *Times and Seasons*, 1 July 1844, p. 575. Other poems by Eliza R. Snow which touch on the martyrdom include "To Elder John Taylor" and "Lines Written on the Birth of the Infant Son of Mrs. Emma, Widow of the Late General Joseph Smith."

5. *Times and Seasons*, 15 December 1844, p. 751; reprinted from the *Nauvoo Neighbor*.

6. William Hyde Journal, holograph, LDS Church Archives.

7. Nelson W. Whipple Journal, holograph, LDS Church Archives.

8. In Kenneth W. Godfrey et al., *Women's Voices: An Untold Story of the Latter-day Saints* (Salt Lake City: Deseret Book Co., 1982), 140–42.

9. *Times and Seasons*, 1 July 1844, p. 575.

10. *Times and Seasons*, 15 December 1844, p. 751.

11. D&C 21:5.

12. *Times and Seasons*, 1 August 1845, p. 991. Phelps also penned "A Voice from the Prophet," which touches on the martyrdom theme.

13. *Times and Seasons*, 1 January 1845, p. 767.

14. Annette P. Hampshire, "Thomas Sharp and Anti-Mormon Sentiment in Illinois, 1842–1845," *Journal of the Illinois State Historical Society* 72 (May 1979): 82–100.

15. In Godfrey et al., *Women's Voices*, 140–42.

16. *Times and Seasons*, 1 January 1845, p. 767.

17. The familiar messianic references are Isaiah 53:7 and Jeremiah 11:19.

18. *Times and Seasons*, 1 August 1844, 607.

19. *Times and Seasons*, 1 January 1845, p. 767.

20. W. I. Appleby, "Lines Suggested by the Reflections of the Call and Martyrdom of the Prophet and Patriarch of the 'Church of Jesus Christ of Latter Day Saints.'" Joseph and Hyrum Smith, (Murdered in Carthage jail, Hancock, Illinois, by a Mob etc. June 27th AD. 1844), William I. Appleby Journal, p. 224.

21. *Times and Seasons*, 2 September 1844, p. 639.

22. Sarah D. Griffith, Diary and Papers, LDS Church Archives.

The Non-Mormon
Response

3

Mob member's powder horn. The powder horn is inscribed "Warsaw regulators, the end of the polygamist Joseph Smith kilt at Carthage June 27, 1844."

The mob killing of two prisoners incarcerated at Carthage was news. Violence always attracts attention, and murders, especially when the surrounding circumstances are unusual, continue to be grist for the mill of the media. It did not take long for the news to spread, whether by word of mouth or through newspaper accounts: Joseph and Hyrum Smith were dead.

Not surprisingly, those most bitterly opposed to Mormonism were relieved. One can imagine the jeering laughter in taverns and other settings, with words to this effect: "Well, old Joe got just what he deserved." Certainly those who had been calling for just this use of force were satisfied, as were those who participated in it. As they scattered to their different homes, in subsequent private talk among themselves, there were laughing proclamations: "Now they know who runs this country." It was a common assumption that Mormonism would not last.

But such crowing did not continue long. For one thing, those who had been connected with the incident had reason to fear criminal indictment. This included not only the members of the mob who in painted faces had charged Carthage Jail and emptied their guns into the room occupied by the unfortunate prisoners. There were also those who had encouraged them, including editor Thomas Sharp, who had urged that the Mormon problem be solved "with powder and ball."[1] However, fears of being brought to justice, though real, did not prevent some vigorous statements from Sharp, defending the murderers.

Governor Thomas Ford was one of those who strongly denounced the extralegal action that had resulted in the violent deaths of the Smith brothers. No doubt sincere in his general insistence that the law prevail, he also wished to disassociate himself from what had occurred at Carthage. After all, it was he who had given a pledge of security to the prisoners. On 5 July 1844, he wrote to the vigilante Warsaw Committee of Safety:

> When I came to your county I announced the policy by which I intended to be governed. The law was to be my guide; and this you well understand. . . . I successively obtained a vote to sustain me in this course from every troop stationed at Carthage, or who was visiting there. From the detachment of your town and vicinity, who visited Carthage the day before the surrender of the Smiths, I obtained a similar pledge. . . . Upon the whole I cannot too strongly express my indignation and abhorrence of the base and profligate act which has disgraced the State and raised suspicions in the minds of many in regard to my conduct in the matter of the most painful character to my feelings.

Ford further refused to assist in driving the Mormons from Illinois: "I am informed that a design is still entertained at Warsaw of attacking Nauvoo. In this you will not be sustained by myself or the people; it is a part of my policy that you remain quiet, and if you please, watchful, but strictly on the defensive; and I now announce to you that I will not be thwarted in this policy with impunity."[2]

Another reason for muffling the shouts of triumph became clear as reactions from around the country came in. The press and, as far as the press can be seen as providing an accurate picture, the general public did not applaud the killers. Printed comments in the immediate aftermath of the killings included the following: "We regard these homicides as nothing else than murder in cold blood—murder against the plighted faith of the chief magistrate of Illinois—murder of a character so atrocious and so unjustifiable as to leave the blackest stain on all its perpetrators—their aiders, abettors, and defenders" (*O.S. Democrat*). The *St. Louis Evening Gazette* and all the other newspapers of St. Louis denounced the deed, one of them calling it "unprovoked murder." *The Democrat* in Lee County, Iowa, agreed with the St. Louis press: this was "premeditated murder," the perpetrators of which "ought to be ferreted out and dealt with according to the strict sense of the law."[3]

The *Illinois State Register* called the murders "the most disgraceful and cold blooded ever committed in a christian land" and further promised that "every effort will be made to bring the assassins to punishment." The *Quincy Herald* did not think that the actual murderers would ever be identified, but considered the mob's deed "a cold-blooded cowardly act, which will consign the perpetrators if discovered to merited infamy and disgrace." After reporting on several public meetings that passed resolutions in support of Governor Ford, the Quincy editors opined that the general population of Hancock County had not been guilty of the horrendous crime but rather "a few desperate characters." Most Hancock people would "as heartily condemn the killing of the Smiths as we do."[4]

While insisting that only the culprits should be held accountable, these editors were not optimistic about the incident's effect on the future reputation of the state of Illinois. "It will live and be brought up in judgment against us, when the present generation has passed away. . . . The public opinion of the civilized world has been outraged by it, and throughout the United States and in Europe the opprobrium of the transaction will be cast upon our people and State at large. It is a deed that will not soon be forgotten." It was not the Mormons, apparently, who first suggested that the innocent blood of the wronged victims would "stain" the state of Illinois.[5]

The *Bloomington Herald* [Iowa] agreed that "the hitherto fair fame of Illinois has been sullied—blackened—by a deed which casts a

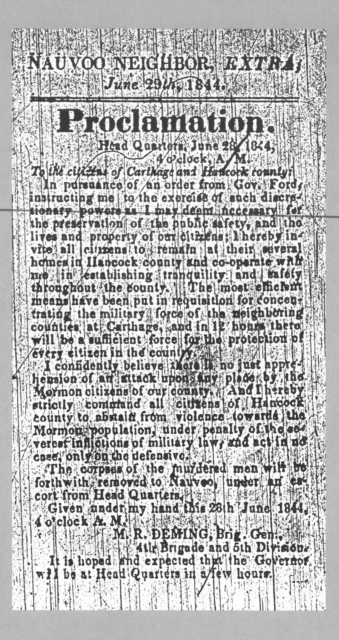

NAUVOO NEIGHBOR, *EXTRA;*
June 29th, 1844.

Proclamation.

Head Quarters, June 28, 1844,
4 o'clock, A. M.

To the citizens of Carthage and Hancock county;

In pursuance of an order from Gov. Ford, instructing me to the exercise of such discretionary powers as I may deem necessary for the preservation of the public safety, and the lives and property of our citizens; I hereby invite all citizens to remain at their several homes in Hancock county and co-operate with me in establishing tranquility and safety throughout the county. The most efficient means have been put in requisition for concentrating the military force of the neighboring counties at Carthage, and in 12 hours there will be a sufficient force for the protection of every citizen in the country.

I confidently believe there is no just apprehension of an attack upon any place by the Mormon citizens of our county. And I hereby strictly command all citizens of Hancock county to abstain from violence towards the Mormon population, under penalty of the severest inflictions of military law, and act in no case, only on the defensive.

The corpses of the murdered men will be forthwith removed to Nauvoo, under an escort from Head Quarters.

Given under my hand this 28th June 1844, 4 o'clock A. M.

M. R. DEMING, Brig. Gen.,
4th Brigade and 5th Division.

It is hoped and expected that the Governor will be at Head Quarters in a few hours.

Proclamation issued by Brigadier General M. R. Deming, ranking officer at Carthage.

stigma upon the whole human family." This editor outdid himself as
he tried to find words to express his disapproval:

> In vain may we search the whole catalogue of crime for an equal to
> this brutal, cowardly, hellish (yes, hellish is the word, but not half
> expressive enough to convey a proper idea of its enormity) murder.
> Assassins may plunge the dagger to the breast of the innocent and
> unsuspecting savages may torture, kill and slay, but these crimes
> are virtues in comparison with the heart of the reputed civilized
> man who in cold blood murders the victim who has voluntarily
> placed himself in the hands of his enemy, to be tried and dealt with
> according to law. Only think of it, a man in the nineteenth century,
> an age of boasted light and reason, voluntarily surrendered as a
> prisoner ready to suffer for his crimes or misdemeanors over-
> powered and slain in cold blood. Language is inadequate to paint
> the outrage in the color it merits. It matters not what may have
> been the misdeeds of Smith, they cannot be offered in palliation of
> this horrid crime, nothing can justify such an outrage.[6]

The *Missouri Republican*, upon hearing the first reports, said: "All
our information tends to fix upon the people concerned in the death
of the Smiths, the odium of perfidious, black-hearted, cowardly murder—as wanton, as to be without any justification—so inhuman and
treacherous, as to find no parallel in savage life under any
circumstances."[7] By mid-July the Lee County *Democrat* [Iowa],
which had expressed its revulsion earlier, repeated its condemnation
of the assassinations at greater length. The murder of the Smiths,
the paper asserted, "has caused feelings of deep regret in the breasts
of every peaceable and law abiding people; they look upon it as a
high handed outrage, and as a cruel, cold blooded, cowardly and
contemptible murder."[8]

This condemnation of the murderers was almost universal,[9] but it must not be misunderstood. It did not represent approval of Joseph Smith or the Mormons. Often the editorial reaction would include disclaimers such as the following from the *Bloomington Herald* [Iowa]: "That Smith was an evil disposed man, dangerous in community, we cannot dispute." Or as the *Democrat* put it: "That Jo and his brother were guilty of acts which required the interposition of the law, we are well aware, but after he and his brother had voluntarily surrendered themselves up to justice, under the full assurance that they would receive the protection of Gov. Ford from all violence, they were entitled to all protection against all danger and all enemies." It was not so much the loss of Joseph Smith as it was the lawless manner of his removal that aroused condemnation.[10]

A large part of the reason for condemning the assassinations, it has been suggested, is that they were seen as yet another example of rioting by a lawless mob. The Carthage debacle occurred in a season of urban violence and mob disturbances throughout the country.[11] The malady was of the generation, with thirty or more riots in Baltimore, Philadelphia, New York, and Boston from the 1830s to the 1850s, as well as numerous individual lynchings.

Eighteen forty-four was a year of intense concern about this rampant lawlessness. The largest outbreak of violence was a series of riots at Philadelphia. In fact, the same newspapers that reported the Nauvoo assassinations described the Philadelphia tumult, and the two incidents, Philadelphia and Carthage, were often linked. The *New York Daily Tribune*, for example, wrote of the martyrdom: "Altogether it is a sad and melancholy business, and will leave a dark spot, side by side with the records of the Philadelphia riots, in the history of these times."[12] Wilford Woodruff mentioned this mob spirit in his own journal just days after his first news of the martyrdom: "Mob spirit is rising through out the Country. Philadelphia is full of it."[13]

In the face of all this indignation and concern about rampant violence, was anyone willing to defend the assassinations? A report by the *Quincy Herald* offers a revealing glimpse: "A man was assailed and knocked down with a musket in Warsaw yesterday, for presuming to express disapprobation at the murder of the Smiths."[14] How many such altercations occurred we have no way of knowing, but it is apparent that Warsaw continued to be a center of anti-Mormon sentiment.

It was in Warsaw especially that the rationale for using violence against the Mormons was most fully articulated and expressed in meetings, resolutions, newspaper articles, and letters. In essence the Warsaw residents' position was that which had been used to justify vigilante or regulator activity elsewhere in the country: the law had proved itself powerless; the perceived offense was so serious that it could not be allowed to continue; and it was the extralegal organization that genuinely represented the popular will. Such had been the basis of Thomas Sharp's inflammatory demand, mentioned earlier, that the Mormon problem be solved "by powder and ball."

Sharp now continued his hammering of the Mormons in the pages of the *Warsaw Signal*. Stung by the nearly universal condemnation of the murders, he published a lengthy article entitled "The Act and the Apology" on 10 July 1844. To understand his line of reasoning it is helpful to itemize the main points:

1. Above the strict law of the land is something higher, variously called the law of God, the law of nature, or "reserved rights." Admitting that the assassinations were outside the law of the land, Sharp considered them justified by an appeal to the higher law of self-defense.

We received the above communication by the hands of CHARLES A. FOSTER about ¼ past 11 o'clock to day. We have only to state, that this is sufficient! War and extermination is inevitable! CITIZENS ARISE, **ONE** and **ALL**!!!— Can you *stand* by,—and suffer such IN- FERNAL DEVILS! to rob men of their property and RIGHTS, without avenging them. We have no time for comment, every man will make his own. LET IT BE MADE WITH **POWDER AND BALL**!!!

We take the following, from an extra of the Nauvoo Neighbor. It shows the the devils in their proper light.

Thomas Sharp's infamous "powder and ball" statement, from the Warsaw Signal, 12 June 1844.

2. Joseph Smith "and his minions," in Sharp's estimation, had been guilty of theft, counterfeiting, and physical and verbal abuse.

3. The law had proven itself incapable of bringing Joseph Smith to justice: "The Mormon community were leagued together, and judging from their acts, it appeared to be a part of their religion to fleece, insult and rob the Gentiles, as non believers are by them called, and then to stand by and protect each other from legal punishment."

4. Smith's actions had become increasingly presumptuous. Sharp was especially exercised by the destruction of the press (the *Nauvoo Expositor*) and putting the city of Nauvoo under martial law.

5. Though the Smiths had been arrested, their just condemnation was not assured. Answering those who insisted that the law should have been allowed to run its course, Sharp argued that "the course of the law in the case of these wretches would have been a mere mockery." This argument was twofold. First, the prisoners would probably have escaped. Second, even if they had not escaped, they would have gone free. This was explained quite simply by the fact that Mormons were a majority in the county. "Last year he [Smith] selected one of his miserable cat's paws for County Commissioner; at the next August election, he would have selected another, which would have given him the complete control of the County Commissioner's Court. This Court selects the Grand and Petit Jurors; or in other words Joe Smith would through them have chosen; first the men who could alone bring him to trial, and secondly, the jury before whom he would be arraigned."

6. It was better that these two leaders, "the instigators and authors of all our troubles," be killed than to have a war in which many would suffer. Sharp asked:

Is it not better that the blood of two guilty wretches, whose crimes had long awaited the vengeance of Heaven, has been shed and thus by cutting off the fountain head to dry up the stream of corruption; or would it have been better that they had escaped, as they inevitably would have done through the meshes of the law, and thus brought on a conflict, in which not only hundreds of valuable lives would have been lost, but the blood of the innocent mingled with that of the guilty?

7. Backed by these arguments, the action could be considered courageous and noble. Like other vigilantes, Sharp compared himself and his associates to the freedom fighters of the American Revolution. "No man through whose veins courses one drop of that noble blood, which prompted our forefathers to throw off the yoke of British oppression, will ask his fellow freeman to kneel at the nod of any tyrant, nor condemn him for asserting his liberty, even if in so doing he is obliged to commit a daring violation of law."

Incredibly, Sharp concluded by claiming that "the community in which we live, is a law abiding community, and that it will go as far to maintain the supremacy of the law as any other in the nation. Our citizens have regretted, and still regret the necessity that existed for taking the law in this particular instance, into their own hands."[15]

One week later, on 17 July 1844, a lengthy article by Sharp reviewed the whole sequence once again. Regarding the promise made to Joseph and Hyrum Smith that they would be safe, Sharp wrote: "[T]hey had the promise of the Governor's protection; this was not well, and we think was not generally known, until his Excellency proclaimed it after the catastrophe." Sharp put himself in the minds of "the old citizens" of Hancock County. What satisfaction could they have in knowing that Joseph Smith was in jail? Didn't Joseph and Hyrum deserve to die? "Evidence enough to damn them forty times over, has been published. Read the history of the Missouri investigation—Bennet's, Harris, Howe's and Tucker's words, the multitude of affidavits which have been published." These anti-Mormon works were accepted without question by Sharp. Knowing that "the law could not reach" the Smiths, what would the "old citizens" naturally conclude? "They chose a bitter alternative— one revolting to their own sensibilities, but prompted by a high sense of duty to themselves and their Country. . . . it had to be done then and there or not at all." In a ringing declaration, Sharp proclaimed, "We plead the necessity of the case."

Although the overwhelming weight of newspaper opinion had denounced the murderers, the Warsaw anti-Mormons did gain some support. George T.M. Davis, editor of the *Alton Telegraph* [Illinois], wrote that he could not approve of mob violence, but if ever there was justification for such behavior, this was it. The Mormons had been disliked wherever they had lived. They had become very numerous, threatening to control the state at the ballot box. The Mormon community was "a compound of ignorance and villainy— the mass falling under the class of ignorance; while nine tenths of all the principal men, and their immediate instruments, are most justly to be enumerated as villains and desperadoes of the deepest dye." Nauvoo was a refuge for criminals. The Mormons controlled Hancock County offices and thus could prevent the execution of justice through the courts. By itemizing a series of outrages, told from the point of view of the anti-Mormons, editor Davis left little doubt as to where his sympathies lay. Noticing the frequency of mob violence in American cities, he drew the conclusion that cities where such has occurred "should seal their lips against condemning the citizens of Carthage and Warsaw." In the fall of 1844, Davis expanded his article into a pamphlet entitled *An Authentic Account of the Massacre of Joseph Smith, the Mormon Prophet and Hyrum Smith, His Brother.*[16]

When another editor at the *Alton Telegraph*, a Mr. Bailhache, condemned the assassins, Thomas Sharp's long, sarcastic response repeated much of the argument itemized above. Bailhache insisted that mob violence was never excusable, that a pledge of honor had been given for the protection of the prisoners, and that the "powerless" prisoners, if guilty, would have been duly convicted and punished. "Now friend Bailhache," Sharp countered, "if you are so scrupulously good as to suffer a bloody villain to cut your own throat, or the throats of your friends, and for fear of violating the law will not consent to resort to the only means left you to prevent such a state of things, and, seize the only opportunity that probably ever would have been presented, to remove the wretches who would inevitably bring about all these evils, we can only say, that you are a better christian than we ever expect or desire to be."[17]

With rare exceptions, this rationalization of vigilante lynching was not accepted. Of course the Mormons insisted that the martyrdom was murder and demanded punishment.[18] But almost all other newspapers reacted with the same insistence. The *New York Herald* considered Sharp's defense of the murders "a gratuitous justification of cold-blooded murder." Even granting all of his premises, the fact remained, said the *Herald*, that Sharp was appealing to violence instead of the law.[19]

The *New York True Sun* again raised the question of what the murders would mean for the honor of Illinois: "The honor of the State of Illinois, already equivocal in pecuniary affairs, will have the stain of blood upon it, if the murderers be not brought to condign punishment." In the eyes of this editor, the perpetrators were "a gang of cowardly cut-throats, every one of whom is as worthy of the gallows as any pirate that ever swung."[20]

Whether the murderers would be brought to justice would be determined in the Illinois courts. In *Carthage Conspiracy* modern scholars Dallin H. Oaks and Marvin S. Hill have produced a thorough study of "the trial of the accused assassins of Joseph Smith."[21] They describe the efforts to prevent Sheriff Minor Deming from arresting the murderers; the "deal" made by Governor Ford with two of the accused, Thomas Sharp and Levi Williams; the selection of a grand jury with no Mormons (despite their predominance in the population); the indicting of nine men, four of whom never appeared for trial; the selection of a jury that again excluded all Mormons; and the subsequent trial of the remaining five accused before a crowd of anti-Mormon spectators. When the prosecuting attorney excluded the testimony of his three most telling witnesses, and when defense attorneys emphasized the widespread sentiment against the Smiths and the need of an acquittal in order to preserve the peace, the verdict was a foregone conclusion. In essence, the anti-Mormon rationale already spelled out in Thomas Sharp's newspaper, that of popular sovereignty and reserved rights, was accepted in the court.

The mob succeeded in escaping justice for the murders of Joseph and Hyrum; however, if they thought that the end of the Prophet Joseph meant the end of Mormonism, they were wrong. Though the idea was entertained—for example, in the *New York Herald*, whose article was headlined "Thus Ends Mormonism!"[22]—it was not the standard response. It quickly became obvious both inside and outside of the Church that the loss of their leader would not cause the Mormons to give up or scatter.

Following this line of reasoning, the editor of the *Philadelphia Sun* made the inevitable comparison with Mohammed:

[S]ince the time of the Arabian Mahomet, there never were circumstances in the history of a religious sect, so propitious to the establishment and wide spread increase of its votaries, as there are now exhibited in the history of the Mormon sect. The manner and circumstances of Mr. Smith's death, have invested his cause with a dignity, and have infused an element of success, greater than its most devoted friends could have anticipated.

There wants nothing but a deep conviction of the truth of the Mormon doctrine to animate a dozen of Smith's adherents to set out on a mission from the scene of their prophet's martyrdom, and effects of the most astounding character in the religious world must necessarily follow.

Nauvoo and Carthage will become the Mecca and Medina of the Mormon Prophet, and thousands of devotees may be drawn to make holy pilgrimages to the scenes of the prophet's labors and of his death.[23]

This non-Mormon author was confident of the future: "Mormonism has just commenced its career. It will date its greatest triumphs from the massacre at Carthage Prison."

Horace Greeley, of the *New York Tribune*, was another who did not assume that the death of its prophet would mean the end of Mormonism. As he explained:

Gross and monstrous as the delusions and perhaps the abominations practiced in the name of that faith, yet it is a vital, living thing. Men and women made of the same sort of flesh and blood and actuated by similar sensations and passions, as Protestants, Catholics, Mohammedans, or whatsoever creed or worship the sun shines upon, do actually *believe* in this Mormonism—are content to live and die by it—to yield up worldly wealth, domestic ties, and the strong bonds of love of Native land, for it and thus feeling and thus believing, to their dimned and distorted spiritual vision Joe Smith is as much the Martyr Hero as any whose shadow has ever fallen upon the world. The blood of Joe Smith, spilled by murderous hands, will be like the fabled dragon's teeth sown broadcast, that everywhere sprang up armed men.

He counseled the Saints to "bide their time," to which the Nauvoo editor responded: "Well said, Mr. Greeley. Pure religion always did 'bide its time'."[24]

A recognition that such persecution and killing produced martyrs was also noted by the *Plough-boy* of Mt. Carmel, Illinois:

Who knows but what Carthage of Illinois, will yet become as noted in history as is its ancient namesake, of Punic memory. Joe and his brother Hyrum, will be looked upon as martyrs, by the Latter day Saints; and in their future church history, Carthage will figure, as the place where died the Prophet by the hands of the ungodly—hope it may be the only one, whom they may, with some degree of propriety chronicle as such—hope that all the rest of the Mormons may die in their beds, as good christians ought to; and we yet again hope, that hereafter the Mormons may be judged by our laws and punished accordingly, and not by our muskets, in the hands of those, who are ever ready to commit outrage, when tumult and excitement give them a probable chance of doing so with impunity. We may expect that Fanaticism will flourish more and more if we but manage to persecute it a little now and then.[25]

A similar analysis appeared in the pages of the *Tompkins Democrat* [New York]:

"This is the end of Mormonism," is the exclamation of many editors on announcing the death of Joseph Smith. We differ with them. The doctrines inculcated by him would soon have yielded to the light of reason, had he lived; but now that he has sealed them with his blood, he will be looked upon as a martyr; and how feeble a thing is reason, to combat religious error, when it has become impossible for the prophet and high priest of that error to recant and acknowledge its falsity—when, indeed, he has laid down his life in the defence of it.

Although condescending, this editor was one of the few who had positive words to say about the dead prophet: "Disguise it how we may, a great man has fallen; and among the extraordinary characters of the age—those who have risen from the lowest walks of life, to be 'rulers among men,' history will record the name of JOSEPH SMITH."[26]

While recognizing that most of his colleagues condemned the murders, the *Tompkins Democrat* editor did not hold the press guiltless. He noted that the *Inquirer*, for example, "after contributing its efforts to bring about these appalling murders by publishing every lie that has been promulgated against the Mormons, cries out 'Horrible! we can scarce credit the account.'"[27]

The assassinations and the public reaction cannot be understood in isolation. They represent only one phase in the longstanding persecution of the Mormons and demands for their expulsion or extermination, which stretched back to at least 1833 in Missouri and would continue after Joseph Smith's death. Much of the anti-Mormon case against Smith had been an attack on the religion he founded as something contemptuous and incompatible with normal, respectable society. Those arguments, for whatever they are worth, would continue to be voiced by the persecutors who drove the Mormons from Illinois and by other opponents later.

Our purpose here is to uncover what non-Mormons thought and said about the martyrdom, not to evaluate the overall hostile attitudes and persecution.[28] We can summarize the non-Mormon reaction to the martyrdom as follows: Among the militant anti-Mormons in Illinois it was an act justified by the exigencies of the situation, which rationalization would now be used to justify the continued persecution of the Mormons and their forced exodus from the state. For others in Illinois and the rest of the country, to judge from the broad spectrum of newspaper coverage, the murders were a cowardly, lawless act and an example of a widespread resorting to violence which all right-thinking Americans must deplore. Their admiration for the victims was reserved at best, but their observations on the power of this event in the minds of the Mormon people was astute: the Carthage mob had made two martyrs.

NOTES

1. *Warsaw Signal,* 12 June 1844

2. Ford to the Warsaw Committee, 10 July 1844, reprinted in the *Nauvoo Neighbor*; and in *Journal History,* 3 July 1844.

3. These newspaper reactions are drawn from the *Nauvoo Neighbor,* 10 July 1844. The *Neighbor* made an effort to publish all such statements. Another summary of many newspaper reactions was published in the *Lee County Democrat,* 29 June 1844. See also Larry C. Porter, "How Did the U.S. Press React When Joseph and Hyrum Were Murdered?" *Ensign* 14 (April 1984): 22–23.

4. *Nauvoo Neighbor,* 10 July 1844.

5. That honor might belong to Governor Thomas Ford, whose letter immediately after the martyrdom reviewed his guarantee of protection: "The pledge of security of the Smiths, was not given upon my individual responsibility. Before I gave it, I obtained a pledge of honor by an unanimous vote from the officers and men under my command, to sustain me in performing it. If the assassination of the Smiths was committed by any portion of them, they have added treachery to murder, and have

done all they could do to disgrace the State, and sully the public honor!" *Nauvoo Neighbor*, 14 August 1844.

6. *Nauvoo Neighbor*, 10 July 1844.

7. *Nauvoo Neighbor*, 10 July 1844.

8. *Nauvoo Neighbor*, 17 July 1844.

9. ". . . most of the newspaper press of our country has condemned the assassination of General Joseph and Hyrum Smith as a cowardly, cold blooded murder." *Nauvoo Neighbor*, 7 August 1844. The best evidence comes from Thomas Sharp's acknowledgment that "the summary execution" of the Mormon leaders "has brought upon us the severest censure of nearly the whole newspaper press, as far as we have yet heard. From the almost unanimous expression, of the papers that have reached us, we doubt not, that the same indignant cry of 'cold blooded murder,' will be echoed from one extreme of our wide spread Union to the other." *Warsaw Signal* (Ill.), 10 July 1844, p. 2.

10. *Nauvoo Neighbor*, 10 July 1844.

11. The information and analysis in this paragraph are based on Paul D. Ellsworth, "Mobocracy and the Rule of Law: American Press Reaction to the Murder of Joseph Smith," *BYU Studies* 20, 1 (Fall 1979): 71–82.

12. Ellsworth, "Mobocracy," 78.

13. Wilford Woodruff Journal, 13 July 1844, LDS Church Archives; published in Scott G. Kenney, ed., *Wilford Woodruff's Journal*, 9 vols. (Midvale, Utah: Signature Books, 1983). See also the *Nauvoo Neighbor*, 10, 24, and 31 July; 7 and 14 August.

14. *Warsaw Signal*, 10 July 1844.

15. *Nauvoo Neighbor*, 7 August 1844.

16. George T. M. Davis, *An Authentic Account of the Massacre of Joseph Smith, the Mormon Prophet and Hyrum Smith, His Brother, Together With a Brief History of the Rise and Progress of Mormonism and all the Circumstances Which Led To Their Death* (St. Louis: Chambers and Knoff, 1844).

17. *Warsaw Signal*, 10 July 1844, p. 3.

18. *Nauvoo Neighbor*, 7 August 1844.

19. *Nauvoo Neighbor*, 25 September 1844.

20. *Nauvoo Neighbor*, 7 August 1844.

21. Dallin H. Oaks and Marvin S. Hill, *Carthage Conspiracy: The Trial of the Accused Assassins of Joseph Smith* (Urbana: University of Illinois Press, 1975).

22. *New York Herald*, 7–8 July 1844.

23. *Nauvoo Neighbor*, 14 August 1844.

24. *Nauvoo Neighbor*, 24 July 1844.

25. *Nauvoo Neighbor*, 31 July 1844.

26. *Nauvoo Neighbor*, 7 August 1844.

27. *Nauvoo Neighbor*, 14 August 1844. The Mormon editor liked this analysis: "The writer understands his subject and tells the truth."

28. See Leonard J. Arrington and Davis Bitton, *The Mormon Experience: A History of the Latter-day Saints* 2nd ed. (Urbana: University of Illinois Press, 1992), ch. 2; and Davis Bitton, *Images of Joseph Smith*, forthcoming.

The Martyrdom in
Later Prose and Poetry

"The Martyred,"
by Gary Smith (oil on
canvas).

Efforts to capture the martyrdom in words—diaries, letters, poetry—did not stop in 1844 or 1850, of course. Writers, scholars, and artists, both in and out of the Church, continued to try to make sense of, pay homage to, and understand more fully the men and events of Carthage on the afternoon of 27 June 1844. Thus accounts of the martyrdom continued to make their way into numerous ostensibly factual narrations—in newspapers, histories, or biographies—and contemporary writers of fiction and poetry still find inspiration in the tragic death of the Prophet and his brother.

Most of the histories that appeared in the second half of the nineteenth century relied rather closely on the firsthand accounts that had been published immediately following the martyrdom. Willard Richards, for example, had published his own eyewitness account, "Two Minutes in Jail," within a month of the event.[1] After some initial confusion among some of the newspapers, the press had conveyed a basically accurate picture of the sequence of events.[2] The *why* question, which included assigning guilt and interpreting a maze of background factors, was not so easily resolved or often undertaken.

In 1845, William M. Daniels published a pamphlet entitled *A Correct Account of the Murder of Generals Joseph and Hyrum Smith*, which was widely distributed and got many of the events straight in their sequence.[3] Unfortunately, although Daniels was at the jail, he proved to be an unreliable witness. He embellished his account, making up things that did not occur and providing the questionable details to Lyman O. Littlefield, who actually wrote the pamphlet. The pamphlet's most striking and perhaps widespread fiction was the account of the moments after Joseph had been shot at the window and fallen to the ground outside the jail:

The ruffian . . . who set him against the well-curb, now secured a bowie-knife for the purpose of severing his head from his body. He raised the knife and was in the attitude of striking, when a light, so sudden and powerful, burst from the heavens upon the bloody scene, (passing its vivid chain between Joseph and his murderers,) that they were struck with terrified awe and filled with consternation. This light, in its appearance and potency, baffles all powers of description. The arm of the ruffian, that held the knife, fell powerless; the muskets of the four, who fired, fell to the ground, and they all stood like marble statues, not having the power to move a single limb of their bodies.[4]

When Daniels appeared as a witness at the trial of some of the alleged murderers, he retracted many of the details, showed himself to be very careless with the facts, and admitted that Littlefield had written the pamphlet. However, tales of the miraculous, especially if they seem faith-promoting, are more easily started than retracted, and the story of the miraculous divine light, which has no basis in fact, continues to be retold.

In *The Rise and Fall of Nauvoo*, published in 1900, the Church's noted early historian, B. H. Roberts, chose to simply repeat the first-hand account given by Willard Richards, though he could not refrain from an editorial appendage to his summary: "Three minutes after the attack was commenced, Hyrum Smith lay stretched out the floor of the prison dead, Elder Taylor lay not far from him savagely wounded, the Prophet was lying by the side of the well curb, just under the window from which he had attempted to leap, the plighted faith of a State was broken, its honor trailed in the dust, and a stain of innocent blood affixed its escutcheon, which shall remain a disgrace forever."[5]

To his credit, Roberts exhibited appropriate skepticism regarding the supposed miracle recounted in the Daniels pamphlet of 1845. "It is worthy of note," wrote Roberts, "that nothing of all this is recorded by Willard Richards, and it smacks too much of the fanciful."

In his later *Comprehensive History*, Roberts has several chapters relating to the martyrdom. His chapter headings give the sense of the content: "The Rising Storm of Mobocracy," "Preliminary Steps to Martyrdom," "The Martyrdom," "Aftermath of the Carthage Tragedy." His description of the events on 27 June is essentially a repeat of his earlier description, reworked slightly to give it something of a breathless tone and forward momentum:

> How quickly disastrous things happened! Three minutes after the attack was commenced upon the jail, Hyrum Smith lay stretched upon the floor of the prison—dead; John Taylor lay not far from him savagely wounded; the Prophet was lying outside the jail by the old well curb—dead; the mob in consternation and disorder had fled in the direction of Warsaw; the plighted faith of a state was broken, its honor trailed in the dust, and a stain of innocent blood affixed to its escutcheon that will remain a blot which time cannot efface.[6]

A note at the end of his chapter is entitled "Did Joseph Smith Make Masonic Appeal for Help." Appropriately cautious, Roberts writes that he "can form no adequate or positive opinion."[7]

Future authors would rely on the firsthand reports penned and chronicled throughout the late nineteenth and early twentieth century in retellings of the martyrdom in a more popular and sometimes speculative realm. For example, 1952 brought the appearance of N.B. Lundwall's *The Fate of the Persecutors of the Prophet*

Joseph Smith. Frankly adulatory, this book included several chapters of background to the 1844 events. These are followed by successive chapters on "Personal Farewells of the Prophet to His Friends," "The Martyrdom" (a blow-by-blow recounting), "The Prophet's Body not Permitted to be Mutilated," "Comments of Friends and Foes on the Martyrdom," "Preparation and Funeral of the Martyrs," "The Sorrow and Mourning of the Saints." Two chapters treat "The Identity and Trial of the Murderers" and "Physical and Mental Suffering of Persecutors." An uncritical compilation, *The Fate of the Persecutors* is not all bad, for it does preserve much primary material. But it unfortunately perpetuates the William Daniels story of the miracle outside the jail and revels in detailing the horrible fate of the persecutors.[8] Already suspect, both of these "faith-promoting" additions to history were decisively exploded by Dallin H. Oaks's and Marvin S. Hill's *Carthage Conspiracy* in 1975.

Also in the 1950s, a journalist named Jim Bishop wrote bestsellers about *The Day Lincoln Was Shot* and *The Day Christ Died*.[9] Probably recognizing a winning idea, Henry Smith, an editor at the *Church News*, prepared a book entitled *The Day They Martyred the Prophet*, published by Bookcraft in 1963.[10] Ten years later, with Henry Smith's book no longer in print, the same publisher brought out a similar treatment, Reed Blake's *24 Hours to Martyrdom*.[11] Neither book provides documentation, and although Blake appends a bibliography, it is insufficient for tracing specific references. Smith provides more context by not limiting himself to twenty-four hours. Neither goes into much depth, but both are conscientious retellings.

Although Lundwall's work is a compilation, a kind of scrap-book, while Smith and Blake provide a single narrative, all three of these works sought to bring a moving, faith-promoting story to the general reader. Critical readers might gain something from the varying perspectives, but clearly these were treatments intended for the believing audience.

Fawn Brodie's *No Man Knows My History* (1945), although controversial, was recognized for its literary excellence. Writing in the tradition of Catherine Drinker Bowen, mixing historical details with the novelist's license, Brodie narrates the events with skill. She feels free to read minds ("Joseph must have felt . . ."), picks the specific quotations that coincided with her interpretation, and is probably sufficiently accurate for most readers. She maintains a breathless momentum in narrating the shooting of the Prophet from inside, his fall from the window, his placement against the well-curb, and the final "execution" as four men shoot him at the orders of Colonel Levi Williams of the Warsaw militia.

Brodie is less than critical in including the miracle of the light that prevented Joseph's decapitation, but at least she clearly designates her source ("To William Daniels it seemed . . ."). Latter-day Saints will never be able to accept her general interpretation of Joseph Smith, for in essence it proclaims him a self-deluded fraud, but her book contains specific passages, like her description of the events at Carthage, that are relatively "neutral" in that they are not necessarily connected to the legitimacy of Joseph's prophetic calling.

Donna Hill's *Joseph Smith: The First Mormon* (1977) had the benefit of a generation of scholarship since the mid-1940s. But she does not resolve the contradictions on some of the details: the number of times Joseph Smith's revolver fired, the number of times his shots reached their mark, how he reached the well, and the moment of death. She leaves out the order of Levi Williams, the close-range execution by four militia men, and also, more defensibly, the miraculous light.[12]

Donna Hill's interpretation of Joseph Smith leaves room for recognizing the legitimacy of his calling, but her telling of the martyrdom events is evenhanded. She does not try to cast the event as a mystery play. Both Brodie's and Hill's books are well researched, considering the sources available when they were written, but written in a style to appeal to a fairly broad audience. They demonstrate, and others will no doubt continue to demonstrate, that even serious histories and biographies can treat the martyrdom differently, by selectivity and emphasis if not by tone, tacit assumptions, implications, or explicit conclusion.

The detailed sequence of events surrounding the martyrdom having been established with as much certainty as seemed possible, the external facts have become familiar. General histories of Mormonism, even biographies of Joseph Smith, while giving their own competent narrations of the Prophet's death have found it less and less necessary to go into so much detail. But it is not only historians who preserve the collective memory of a people. To discover how the martyrdom has been imagined and remembered, as well as how it continues to be perceived, we have also to consider how it has been presented by novelists and poets one hundred and more years after the fact.

When Vardis Fisher published *Children of God: An American Epic* in 1939, many Latter-day Saints were scandalized.[13] Earthy, showing the early Saints in all their humanity, with incorrect grammar and profanity issuing from the mouths of revered leaders, the book certainly did not read like a typical Sunday School manual. Yet Fisher was an American novelist of considerable stature. If he had abandoned the Mormon identity of his childhood, he had not necessarily repudiated all of his earlier beliefs. And clearly he could portray Mormons with sympathy.

Fisher's version of the martyrdom is graphic. Rapid-fire dialogue is exchanged between the characters, and we witness the men in the cell being gunned down with flying bullets.

John went to a window and looked out. Suddenly he cried, "Great God, see!"

The other prisoners ran to the window. A huge mob was coming, a howling horde with blackened faces, with cudgels and knives and guns in their hands. They poured down the street in a great tide. A moment later, there was a sound of profaning men on the stairway outside the cell; and remembering that there was no lock on the door, Joseph sprang to it and the other men followed. They hurled their combined weight to the door and fought with all their strength to keep it closed. Joseph had hidden a small pistol in his clothes. While shouldering against the door, he slipped a hand down to the gun and cocked it. Under the pressure from without, the door shook on its hinges, and four men fought desperately against it with the strength of giants.

A voice yelled: "Come out of there, you Mormon sons-of-bitches!"

For a moment there was silence. Then a man cried with an oath: "I'll shoot them through the door!"

In the next instant a ball splintered a panel of the door and buried itself in the opposite wall. Joseph and John leapt to one side. Hyrum started across the room but had taken only two steps when a second ball struck his nose. He spun and fell with a cry; and as he fell, a third ball plowed through his flesh and lodged deep in his side. He struck the floor and turned convulsively. After a swift glance at his brother, Joseph sprang to the door and opened it far enough to thrust the muzzle of his pistol through. He fired blindly at the howling mob; and while he was desperately pulling the trigger, another bullet crashed through the door and made a gaping wound in Hyrum's throat. A half-dozen barrels were shoved through. These John wildly beat down with a club.

The next few minutes were nightmare for everyone but Joseph. John ran to a window to look out. A ball tore through one of his legs and turned him half-around, and a second bullet smashed his watch. As he fell, a third struck his thigh and blew off a piece of flesh as large as a man's palm. Willard was insanely clubbing the musket barrels as they were shoved through.

Some details may be questioned in this version, but it does capture the frenzy of the moment. With the novelist's license, Fisher concludes by having Joseph experience a feeling of resignation:

Suddenly, while John and Willard were fighting like wild men, Joseph felt deep peace. Like lightning the thoughts came to him that he had known, for many long years, that he must eventually seal his ministry with his blood; that this was the end. He drew to his fullest height for a moment, no longer expecting to escape, no longer afraid. Then slowly he walked to the window. At the moment when he looked out, two bullets entered his breast. They spun him around and left him reeling over the sill.

"O Lord, my God!" he said. His hands sought something to grasp and found nothing; and in the next instant he pitched headlong to the street. Seeing him fall, a Carthage Gray ran up with fixed bayonet. With the point at Joseph's throat, he leaned forward to look at the face. He stepped back.

There was no need to drive with the bayonet. The Prophet was dead.[14]

Again, judged strictly as history, we might quibble with the final sentences, for this fails to mention how Joseph was dragged to the well, propped up, and then fired at. But the tempo seems right. As a literary telling of the final moments at Carthage Jail, Fisher's has to be considered at or near the top.

Another work of historical fiction (or fictionalized history) that includes the Carthage scene is Samuel W. Taylor's, *Nightfall at Nauvoo* (1971). Again this author exercises some of the novelists's prerogative of imagination to capture both the events and a feeling in the air. As John Taylor sings "A Poor Wayfaring Man of Grief" verse by verse, descriptive detail accumulates and tension mounts. In an inspired touch, Samuel Taylor has the religious song inside the jail balanced by a menacing antiphonal choir from outside:

> Hoofbeats drummed outside from a body of riders. Willard, looking out the window, saw only glimpses of movement through the trees screening the next street. It was too soon for Governor Ford's company to be returning. And it was not the Legion, for as they road the man sang a parody of the "Hebrew Children."
>
> > Where now is the Prophet Joseph?
> > Where now is the Prophet Joseph?
> > Where now is the Prophet Joseph?
> > Safe in Carthage Jail!
>
> Willard exchanged glances with Joseph and Hyrum. There could be no question now that the mob was forming.

The description continues blow by blow, as it were, concluding after the death of Joseph and Hyrum. Two of the mobsters are looking for Willard Richards and John Taylor when they are interrupted:

A heavy voice bawled from the lower hallway. "Clean out, men! The Mormons are coming!"

The boots fled downstairs. Conscious of the enormity of the act, the mob divided into individual men again, each horror-stricken at what he'd done. As individuals they fled outside and to the woods to hide.

As graphic description, with mounting tension and release, this is compelling. For both Fisher and Taylor, Joseph Smith was not an icon to adulate but a human being to describe credibly. Neither attempted to turn his description into testimony. The antiseptic Sunday School presentation was not for them, but, considering the range of possible interpretations, their versions are still sympathetic.

Finally, among the most substantial Mormon historical novels is Orson Scott Card's *Saints*, first published in 1984.[15] Card knows how to tell a story. Like Fisher, he freely takes the reader into the mind and thoughts of his protagonist.

The men on the stairs began to shout. Terrible oaths and threats. I ought to be contemplating the glory of God. At least having a vision. That's what prophets are supposed to do when they're about to die. The door pushed back open slowly despite Willard's weight against it.

Hyrum is shown holding the pistol but not using it. Then he is shot and Joseph runs to him.

Joseph eased Hyrum to the ground. It wasn't supposed to be this way. Something had gone wrong. Joseph was supposed to die, not Hyrum. Hyrum was supposed to succeed him at the head of the Church. Wasn't that what Joseph had planned? He took the pistol out of Hyrum's hand. The handle was sweaty. It was still cocked. Hyrum never did them any harm at all, Joseph thought, not even to defend himself. Didn't they know who their enemy was? I am their enemy. And he strode to the door, which was being forced open again, and discharged the pistol six times.

Moments later, Joseph notices that only Willard Richards had found a protected spot behind the door. Again, thoughts rush through his mind in rapid sequence:

Why was everyone standing there, waiting? Why had everything stopped? Were they leaving it up to him again? Was everything going to stay as it was until he moved and changed it? Even now, did they have to depend on him to take charge of his own death? All right, then. He threw the empty pistol to the ground and ran to the window. You want Joseph Smith? Here I am. Not hiding from you in a room. You don't have to come in and get me. I'll come out to you.

He had one foot on the sill when a bullet struck him in the other leg, knocking it out from under him. Don't be so impatient, I'm coming. He lay on the sill, straddling it, one arm and leg outside. He felt the bullets pierce him on both sides, as if some were trying to push him out, the others push him in. Out, he decided, and felt himself slide from the sill toward the open space outside. The pain struck him then, and he felt his mouth open as he cried out, "Oh Lord, my God!" He wasn't quite sure himself whether he was giving the Masonic cry of distress or a complaint. The ground came as the most powerful blow he had ever been struck, and he felt himself bounce into the air a little. He tried to raise himself up. Stand up. Arise. Then he realized that his cry had been neither distress nor complaint. It was a greeting.

Even with the generous mind reading and minor errors of detail, such as the firing of the pistol six times in the jail, this is compelling for its drama and psychological slant. The interior monologue captures the uncertainty of a more human, fallible prophet, but Card's belief is revealed in those final four words: "It was a greeting."

Not simple repetition, the novelists' martyrdom, like that of the historian and artist, varies in detail, point of view, pace, and atmosphere. But where the novelists really seem to differ in their portrayals is in their creation of scene and speculations revealed through characterization. Their mobs howl and curse; the room fills with panic; the pace is frenzied. To a greater extent than the earlier historians, the novelists try to get "into the head" of Joseph Smith to explore his possible feelings as a man perhaps even more than a prophet. They try to capture what we don't really know but wonder about and wish we did.

In another dramatic portrayal, the martyrdom made it to the stage during the 1980s when actor Ted Gibbons performed a one-man show entitled "I Witnessed the Carthage Massacre." Playing the role of Willard Richards, Gibbons told his story from Richards's point of view and often employed his exact words but, in the manner made famous and popular by one-man dramatic portrayals of Mark Twain, Harry S. Truman, and Brigham Young, employed creative artistic license. When it was published as a book in 1988, "I Witnessed the Carthage Massacre" became available to Mormon readers.[16]

Where prose falls short of expressing feeling, the overtones of poetry, with the evocative power of rhythm, rhyme, and poetic figures, can be more powerful. As we have seen, the Saints of the past century turned naturally to poetry in the hopes of capturing the deep emotion and significance they felt accompanied the Prophet's death. Twentieth-Century poets have carried on the tradition as a way to bridge the distance and invest the events of the martyrdom with feeling for today.

S. Dilworth Young, a general authority of the Church, published
The Long Road: From Vermont to Nauvoo in 1967. The final "chapter"
of the book is called "The Martyrdom." In it Young quotes the entire
hymn sung in the jail by John Taylor. Then:

> Sing it again. The Prophet
> Made this last request.
> The plaintive words once more
> Rose on the sultry air.
> The love of Christ was in the song,
> The love of man,
> There in that room in Carthage Jail
> On that hot afternoon.

In staccato phrases the poet describes the mobbing:

> They rush the stair.
> They curse; they force
> The door.
> They fire—
> Hyrum is dead upon the
> Floor;
> John Taylor wounded sore;
> And Joseph Smith
> The Prophet is no more.
> His wounds have killed him
> As he fell.
> He's lying at the curb
> Beside the well.[17]

These lines utilize rhyme and some repetition of final consonant
sounds (curse, force), but present no challenge to understanding.

They are sparse and do not reflect the shock or outrage that so many of the early martyrdom poems did. But they do show an acute aware-ness of the dichotomy between good and evil, as the love of Christ and brotherhood in the room are shattered by the cursing mob.

A respected Mormon poet, Clinton F. Larson, might have been expected to write on this theme. In his play *The Mantle of the Prophet* about eight pages are devoted to the martyrdom in dramatic form, including a soliloquy by Joseph Smith, which reads in part:

> Around me, my brethren; though we die
> We do not; to serve the Lord and His Will
> Is like the gift of the nativity, though from that moment
> He strode to the cross and the centuries of redemption.[18]

Larson's poetic drama is too demanding to be widely popular; nevertheless, this is poetry of high order, a brooding reminiscence which provokes contemplation.

Not as well known as it should be, though strong in art and feeling, is Paul Cracroft's Mormon epic *A Certain Testimony*. A long poetic narration of the sequence of events, full of concrete detail, concludes with this:

> Before he reached the open window, two
> Hard-slamming slugs smashed into Joseph's back.
> They spun him to the sill where outside shot
> Crashed home into his breast.
>   "O Lord, my God!"
> He screamed and tumbled out the window, dead
> Or dying, by the time he hit the ground.
> A Carthage Grey, his painted face cracked wide
> With sooty grin, dragged Joseph's sagging corpse

Against the well-curb, where he propped him up.
"You four men there!" his Colonel barked. "That's Joe.
Take careful aim and tell your kids you helped
To finish off the Mormon fraud." They fired
And Joseph Smith jerked once, then moved no more.[19]

Here is history, character, and action compressed into poetry that lends to the events of 27 June 1844 a sense of immediacy, that re-creates them for "now."

Whether the resulting work is simple or epic, the Latter-day Saints continue to return to the martyrdom theme in their poetry. The 1980 collection *Poems of Praise* contains several works relating to the martyrdom.[20] Sandra Petrie's "June 28, 1844," published in 1975, is another good example:

I was not there.
I did not see the wagon
With its silent burden
Climb the hill
And roll into the town.

I did not hear
The creaking of the wagon wheels,
The horses' hooves.
I did not see
The tender brothers' hands reach out
To lift the prophets from the wagon bed,
To bear the husbands through the door,
To lay the sons upon the table there.

I was not there.
I did not share

The anguish of the wives,
The mother's tears.

More than a hundred thirty years
Have gone.
Zion grows.
Prophets lead. Life goes on.
My time is now,
I was not there.
And yet
I cannot quite forget.[21]

Perhaps distance has left contemporary authors feeling more at liberty to reshape and interpret the story of the martyrdom. Or perhaps with no firsthand witnesses left, they are trying to create—or re-create—something of their own, something to speak more directly to present generations.

There is no such thing, of course, as the definitive poetic treatment of such a subject. If we are going to continue to revisit the Carthage assassination scene in imagination, as surely we shall, the last poem will never be written. For as the Prophet Joseph was made alive to the imaginations and hearts of past generations through art, history, and testimony, future Saints will also wish to do him homage, as did W. H. Auden to his friend and mentor in "In Memory of W. B. Yeats," the first stanza of which reads:

He disappeared in the dead of winter:
The brooks were frozen, the airports almost deserted,
And snow disfigured the public statues;
The mercury sank in the mouth of the dying day.
O all the instruments agree
The day of his death was a dark cold day.[22]

NOTES

1. *Nauvoo Neighbor,* 24 July 1844. See also Appendix.

2. Larry C. Porter, "How Did the U.S. Press React When Joseph and Hyrum Were Murdered?" *Ensign* 14 (April 1984): 22–23.

3. William M. Daniels, *A Correct Account of the Murder of Generals, Joseph and Hyrum Smith, at Carthage, On the 27th Day of June, 1844* (Nauvoo, Ill.: J. Taylor, 1845).

4. Daniels, *A Correct Account,* 15, as quoted in Dallin H. Oaks and Marvin S. Hill, *Carthage Conspiracy: The Trial of the Accused Assassins of Joseph Smith* (Urbana: University of Illinois Press, 1975), 89.

5. B. H. Roberts, *The Rise and Fall of Nauvoo* (Salt Lake City: The Deseret News, 1900), 318–19.

6. B. H. Roberts, *Comprehensive History of The Church of Jesus Christ of Latter-day Saints* (Salt Lake City: Corporation of the President, 1930) 2, 286–87.

7. Roberts made one more major scholarly contribution to the martyrdom story. One of B. H. Roberts's most important projects was the publication of Joseph Smith's *History of the Church,* a compilation with its own tortuous history, stretching from original handwritten versions by scribes, to revision and expansion by official historians in the 1850s, to publication in early form in the *Deseret News* and *Millennial Star* and, finally, in the early twentieth century as volumes edited by Roberts. The first six volumes were published between 1902 and 1912. Twenty years later, in 1932, volume 7 appeared, in which Roberts included in chronological order many of the events and documents concerning the martyrdom. The description of the scene at Carthage is John Taylor's—again a firsthand account. Taylor's summary of events is surrounded and supported by many documents, especially letters, which would provide the raw material for future historians and biographers. Joseph Smith, *History of the Church of Jesus Christ of Latter-day Saints* (Salt Lake City: Deseret News, 1932) vol. 7, esp. chs. 9–14.

8. N. B. Lundwall, *The Fate of the Persecutors of the Prophet Joseph Smith* (Salt Lake City: Bookcraft, 1952). For another point of veiw, see Richard C. Poulson, "Fate of the Persecutors of Joseph Smith: Transmutation of an American Myth." *Dialogue: A Journal of Mormon Thought* 11, 4 (Winter 1978): 63–70.

9. Jim Bishop, *The Day Lincoln Was Shot* (New York: Harper, 1955); *The Day Christ Died* (New York: Harper, 1957); *The Day Kennedy Was Shot* (New York: Bantam Books, 1968).

10. Henry Smith, *The Day They Martyred the Prophet* (Salt Lake City: Bookcraft, 1963).

11. Reed Blake, *24 Hours to Martyrdom* (Salt Lake City: Bookcraft, 1973).

12. Donna Hill, *Joseph Smith: The First Mormon* (Garden City, NY: Doubleday, 1977), 409–416.

13. Vardis Fisher, *Children of God: An American Epic* (New York/London: Harper and Brothers, 1939).

14. Fisher, *Children of God,* 297–99.

15. Orson Scott Card, *Saints* (New York: TOR, 1988), 648—50; originally published under the title *A Woman of Destiny* (New York: Berkeley, 1984).

16. Ted Gibbons, *I Witnessed the Carthage Massacre* (Orem, Utah: Keepsake Books, 1988). A sound recording is also available in the Church Library, Salt Lake City.

17. S. Dilworth Young, *The Long Road: From Vermont to Nauvoo* (Salt Lake City: Bookcraft, 1967), 184–85.

18. Clinton F. Larson, The Mantle of the Prophet and Other Plays (Salt Lake City: Desert Book Co., 1966), 4, 7.

19. R. Paul Cracroft, *A Certain Testimony: A Mormon Epic in Twelve Books* (Salt Lake City: Epic West, 1979), 447.

20. Michael Nibley, "June 27, 1844," in Edward L.Hart and Marden J. Clark, eds., *Poems of Praise* (Provo, Utah: Brigham Young University, 1980). In the same volume see also Sally T. Taylor, "Stephen—The Bodyguard After Carthage," and John B. Harris, "To Joseph."

21. *Ensign* 5 (June 1975): 35.

22. "In Memory of W. B. Yeats," in *The Pocket Book of Modern Verse,* ed. Oscar Williams, 3d ed., rev. (New York: Washing Square Press, 1972), 406.

The Carthage
Tragedy Visualized

5

Death masks of Joseph and Hyrum Smith. Joseph's is on the right.

"Representation of the Murder," from William Daniels's A Correct Account of the Murder of Generals Joseph and Hyrum Smith.

The harrowing events of 27 June 1844 would be told and retold in painstaking detail. As Governor Ford tried to piece together what had happened, as the Mormons asked how this *could* have happened, both Willard Richards and John Taylor, eyewitnesses and nearly victims themselves, wrote detailed accounts. In connection with the trial of the assassins, the basic sequence of events was gone over a number of times, and one hundred years later poets and writers would still attempt to capture the drama and significance of the event. Inevitably, visual artists would try their hand at depicting their own perceptions brought on by that afternoon at Carthage.

Although not a picture of the event, two of the earliest visual artifacts related to the martyrdom are the death masks taken of both Joseph and Hyrum Smith. This nineteenth-century practice that has now fallen into disuse was an effort to capture the exact physiognomy of a deceased person at the time of death. Looking at the death masks of the dead prophets, one has an eerie feeling of participating in a moment in history. A bullet wound shows along Hyrum's nose.

The first mass-produced representation of the event, as far as we know, was in the 1845 pamphlet published under the name of William Daniels. As explained in the preceding chapter, this pamphlet recounted that a "ruffian" had been about to cut off Smith's head when he was stunned by a supernatural light. Mobsters assigned to fire at the prophet were temporarily paralyzed. Although at the trial of alleged mob members, witness Daniels recanted almost all of this and showed himself careless of the truth, the story continued to be told and artists did not ignore it.[1]

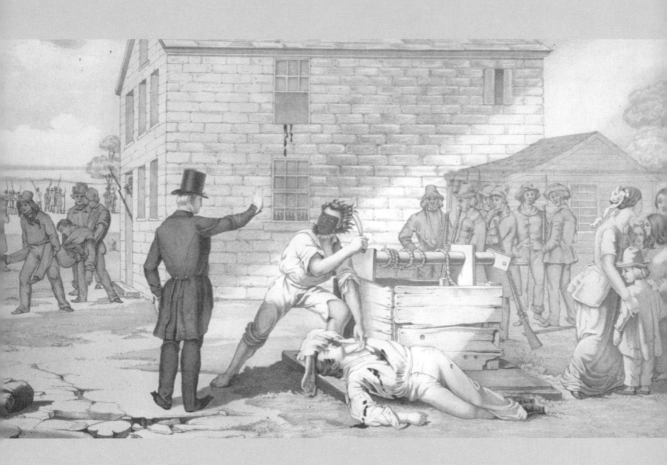

*"Martrydom of Prophet
Joseph Smith."*

Before the days of photography, or before photography could be reproduced in periodicals, the line drawing reproduced by means of an engraving was the standard form by which visual images were mass-produced to the general public. Within seven years of the Daniels drawing, a much more professional engraving had been produced that included some of the Daniels details. This engraving appeared often in books and was even reproduced in a large version suitable for framing. With its availability and drama, one has to wonder how many Mormon—or even non-Mormon—homes were graced with this work hanging on the wall.

"Death of Joseph Smith," from J. H. Beadle's Life in Utah.

"Cruel Assassination of the Prophet Joseph Smith . . ."

Other illustrators turned their hand to the subject of the martyrdom in the second half of the nineteenth century. Many of these drawings appeared as illustrations in historical works and primarily attempted to capture a dramatic moment in history rather than embody an artist's feelings or "message" about the martyrdom. Exterior views tended to show the prophet propped up against the well as members of the mob fire at him, as in "Death of Joseph Smith," which appeared in J. H. Beadle's *Life in Utah*.

The same instant is captured in another engraving, with larger scope and more detail.

"Assassination of Joseph Smith," from T. B. H. Stenhouse's Rocky Mountain Saints.

One of the better representations, "Assassination of Joseph Smith," appears to have been prepared for publication in *Rocky Mountain Saints* by T. B. H. Stenhouse and was then widely reproduced. It captures the instant in time as Joseph is falling from the window of the jail.

Untitled. Artist unknown.

"Murder of Joseph and Hyrum Smith," from The Youths' History of the United States.

Two artists tried to show what was happening from inside the jail. One rather primitive drawing, with the body of Hyrum Smith lying on the floor, is scrupulously accurate in showing Willard Richards behind the door, John Taylor beating at the musket barrels with a club, and Joseph standing with a pistol in his hand.

The second, artistically superior if less exact historically, is almost melodramatic and appeared in *The Youths' History of the United States*, published in 1877.

"Interior of Carthage Jail," from C. C. A. Christensen's Mormon Panorama (tempera on canvas).

"Exterior of Carthage Jail," from C. C. A. Christensen's Mormon Panorama (tempera on canvas).

In addition to these black-and-white engravings, Mormons with an artistic bent sought to preserve some of the vivid scenes of their history, including the martyrdom, in paintings. As early as 1845 William W. Major was at work in Nauvoo painting the martyrdom.[2] Writing to Brigham Young from Winter Quarters, Philo Dibble proposed to expand the number of historical paintings and present them as a panorama to the members of the Church. He went on to do this and certainly had at least one large canvas showing the martyrdom. Unfortunately Major's martyrdom art has not survived.

Also anxious to preserve the first two decades of Mormon history on canvas was C. C. A. Christensen, a Danish convert to the Church. An artist with some formal training, he was prolific for several decades.[3] His series on Church history, which traveled through the Mormon settlements in the West for many years, included two paintings on the martyrdom. One, showing the interior of the jail, carries across the bottom a caption which reads: "The blood of the martyrs is the seed of the Church."

Christensen's exterior scene, not surprisingly, shows the miraculous shaft of light stopping the would-be decapitator dead in his tracks.

Figures in the diorama from the visitors center at Carthage Jail, ca. 1980.

Final scenes from the Church filmstrip "The Martyrdom."

In the twentieth century, there was even a flannel board version of the martyrdom created for use in Sunday School classes. The little figures could be cut from the pages of the *Instructor* magazine and then, with the necessary flannel backing for mounting, be placed on the board as the story was told.[5] The idea was that children needed the visual dimension to help them comprehend what had happened.

The twentieth century saw other developments. To make the scene more interesting and meaningful for visitors, the Church created a diorama at Carthage Jail. For a few years in the 1980s one looked into the room there and saw life-size figures representing Joseph and Hyrum Smith, John Taylor, and Willard Richards caught in a moment of time, probably the evening before the martyrdom, prior to the outbreak of violence.[6]

For instructional purposes in seminaries and institutes, the Church made a filmstrip available in 1966.[7] Part of a series on Church history, the strip on the martyrdom, with accompanying sound, showed many of the details leading up to the murders: meetings of the dissidents in Nauvoo, publication of the *Expositor*, meetings of the city council, the destruction of the newspaper, reaction in neighboring towns, the attempt to arrest Joseph Smith, his brief flight across the river, the return to Nauvoo, the horseback ride to Carthage, meetings with Governor Ford, the imprisonment, nighttime conversations with Dan Jones. The climactic final moments in the jail are shown in detail. Though not great art, these illustrations nevertheless helped the student to visualize the historical events.

*"An Act of Defense,"
by Gary Smith (oil on
canvas).*

*"Panic in the Room,"
by Gary Smith (oil on
canvas).*

A six-minute movie entitled *Last Day at Carthage* became available in 1967. Written and produced by R. Don Oscarson, *Last Day* included no human actors but used black-and-white footage to retrace the route from Nauvoo to Carthage and then, with voice-over narration, to recount the main sequence of the martyrdom itself. There is no telling how many students may have seen this presentation, but in 1990 it was included in a video entitled *Moments from Church History,* which was distributed through Church distribution and subsequently found in homes throughout the Church.[8]

In the twentieth century, too, came the preeminent artist of the martyrdom, Gary Smith. A convert to the Church, Smith recognized the dramatic potential of the assassinations and caught the vision of a highly charged moment in time in which good and evil clashed.[9] Using a simple, primitive style reminiscent of the 1840s, Smith has produced a series of works on the martyrdom. One, "An Act of Defense," shows Joseph in white, standing against the door. Hyrum has just been shot. Intense energy fills the room.

The next work brings the viewer into the room at a precise moment: John Taylor has been hit; Willard Richards tries parrying the intruding rifle barrels with his cane; Joseph, again in white, approaches the window, while outside the jail, members of the mob are visible, rifles pointing upwards.

"Forces of Opposition,"
by Gary Smith (oil on
canvas).

"Spiritual Witnesses,"
by Gary Smith (oil on
canvas).

Another painting shows Joseph lying on the ground, stunned but still alive, surrounded by members of the mob. The light surrounding the white-clad Joseph is in sharp contrast to the dark of the surrounding atmosphere and the mob. Entitled "Forces of Evil," this work leaves no doubt as to the identity of the evil.

This is also true of "Forces of Opposition," a painting which shows Joseph being dragged against the well, where he is shot at point-blank range by four members of the mob. Although artist Smith does not succumb to the temptation to use the discredited Daniels story of attempted decapitation and an angelic intervention, with his use of light and dark and by having the Prophet always clad in white he unhesitatingly displays a clearly delineated confrontation between good and evil. In another work, "Spiritual Witnesses," we discern spirits hovering in the background.

Two final works, "The Martyred" and "Transferring Bodies," complete the cycle.

"Monday, 24 June 1844, 4:15 A.M.," by Pino Drago.

Pino Drago's 1987 painting entitled "Monday, 24 June 1844, 4:15 A.M.," one of the winners in a competition sponsored by the Museum of Church History and Art that year, is another interesting contemporary example that plays on the martyrdom theme but also does much more. Set in time just before the solemn prophet is ushered to Carthage, this work is pregnant with the kind of iconographic meaning usually associated with Renaissance art. As Drago explained, Joseph looks past the viewer and beyond the approaching martyrdom to his future in eternity. Further, one of his hands holds tightly to this life, while the other is relaxed as he faces the next world.[10]

It is doubtful that we have seen the last effort to portray the martyrdom artistically. Like the Annunciation or the Nativity, it is a subject of natural drama that artists—particularly artists within the Church—will continue to be attracted to. The fact that the Annunciation had been painted hundreds of times already did not stop Leonardo da Vinci. One might have concluded that there was nothing new to say artistically about the Crucifixion, but this did not stop Salvador Dali. My own guess is that the most interesting visual representations of the martyrdom will come from Church members schooled in non-Western artistic traditions: Eastern European, Asian, African, or West Indian.

On the other hand, it is worth noting that Mormons as a people have not been attracted to sanguinary art. I do not know the entire reason for this, but suspect that it has to do with nineteenth-century tastes as opposed to earlier centuries of Christian art, and to Protestant (practically all Mormons of the past century came from Protestant backgrounds) as opposed to Catholic, especially Hispanic, tastes in religious art. The most obvious example of this is

*"Room in which Joseph
and Hyrum Smith
Were Imprisoned," by
Frederick Piercy.*

the absence of crucifixes in Mormon chapels or households and the absence of crosses on churches, temples, or anywhere else within Mormonism.

A standard explanation for this has been, "Yes, we recognize the importance of the crucifixion and appreciate Christ's sacrifice, but we prefer to remember him in his living or resurrected state." In other words, it is a question not of theology but of taste, of preference, of just which mental pictures one wishes to focus on. The Latter-day Saints, "like the earliest Christians," writes Roger Keller, "are reluctant to display the cross because they view the 'good news' of the gospel as Christ's resurrection more than his crucifixion."[11]

If this analysis is correct, then it is not too surprising that the martyrdom has not been an obsession with Latter-day Saints. Almost never will you find a painting of the martyrdom hanging in Mormon meetinghouses.

Likewise, Carthage Jail is not a shrine, not a place to which Mormons make pilgrimages. The tourists who go there and find it interesting or stroll pensively through the jail do not genuflect or make other outward displays of pious devotion. It appears that Mormons, rather than dwelling unduly on his moment of final horror, indeed prefer to remember a living Joseph Smith.

All of which may explain why in the Mormon artistic tradition there is the occasional art work on the martyrdom, but much more common are portraits of the living Joseph Smith or paintings of other moments in his life. Even Carthage Jail, the structure itself or pictures of it, can often serve the purpose of recalling the death of the Prophet without all of the gory details. As early as the 1840s an engraving by Frederick Piercy served this purpose.

Present-day grounds at
Carthage Jail.

Those who travel to Carthage now find the jail restored, clean, and proper. The yards are impeccably landscaped, and beautiful flowers and shrubs bloom in spring and summer. Inside the jail friendly Mormon guides, with their inevitable name-tags, explain what happened there. Upon emerging from the prison, amidst the well-groomed grounds and the colorful flowers, one encounters statues of the two martyred brothers showing them not dead but alive.

NOTES

1. In answer to questioning, Daniels said: "Since I have lived in Nauvoo I have exhibited a painting in Nauvoo representing this light and when asked I have told that it was not correct but when not asked I said nothing." Another transcription of this interchange refers to "painters" in the plural. Dallin H. Oaks and Marvin S. Hill, *Carthage Conspiracy: The Trial of the Accused Assassins of Joseph Smith* (Urbana: University of Illinois Press, 1975), 136, 141n.

2. *On the Mormon Frontier: The Diary of Hosea Stout, 1844–1861* 2 vols. (Salt Lake City: University of Utah Press, 1964), 1:25, 56, 61. Glen Leonard, eminent authority on the history of Nauvoo, informs me that William Major may have been assisted by Robert Campbell, a draftsman.

3. Richard L. Jensen and Richard G. Oman, *C. C. A. Christensen, 1831–1912: Mormon Immigrant Artist* (Salt Lake City: The Church of Jesus Christ of Latter-day Saints, 1984).

4. In addition to appearing in Jensen and Oman, *C. C. A. Christensen*, the two martyrdom paintings were reproduced in *Ensign* (December 1979).

5. Marie F. Felt, "It Happened at Carthage Jail." *Instructor* (December 1968): 483–85, 487.

6. A picture of the Carthage Jail Diorama is in the Church Library, Salt Lake City (number 123644).

7. "The Martyrdom." Episode 8—filmstrip multimedia box 2. Copyright 1966 by David O. McKay, copy in Church Library, Salt Lake City.

8. *Moments from Church History* (The Church of Jesus Christ of Latter-day Saints, 1990). The *Last Day at Carthage* segment was produced in 1967. I did notice in it one

inaccuracy, or misleading statement: "Joseph's gun misfired." Actually, three of the six barrels misfired, while the other three not only fired but found their mark.

9. *New Era* 3 (December 1973): 20–30.

10. These descriptions from the labels prepared by the Museum of Church History and Art for the 1992–93 exhibit are based on a letter from the artist.

11. Roger R. Keller, "Cross," in *Encyclopedia of Mormonism*, 4 vols. (New York: Macmillan), 1:344.

E p i l o g u e

What, then, was the meaning of those deaths that occurred so quickly in the afternoon of 27 June 1844? What is the meaning of any human life? The answer lies not in abstract reasoning or legal definition but in the minds of those who survive and remember.

The murderers and their sympathizers saw their victims as bad, insufferable individuals who had to go. Their removal, therefore, was an act of righteous extrajudicial execution representing the will of the larger community. At least this was the publicly stated justification. Just how comfortable each of those involved was with an excuse rejected by most of the country is another question, but we know enough about human responses to suspect that something like this rationalization might have worked as a salve to conscience. Had the event been covered by news reporters from the 1990s, whisked back by some magic time machine, they no doubt would have returned to tell us (as they did following the Los Angeles riots of 1992) that we must "understand the rage" of the murderers at Carthage.

One suspects that many in the mob of 200 might indeed have considered themselves swept along by a crowd psychology of fury, the outcome and implications of which were imperfectly understood. Except for those few whose weapons actually fired into the room from the inside and a few others who were close enough to be sure of their aim from the outside, one can well imagine a response something like this: "I was there, but I didn't kill him."

For the immediate families of Joseph and Hyrum Smith, the significance of the event was a terrible vacancy in their immediate family circle. Theirs was the grief experienced by all human beings as family members die, made more difficult in this instance by the suddenness and the violence of it all. Lucy Mack Smith had lost two sons on 27 June, including the son on whom she had placed great importance as rescuer of the family. Emma Smith was now a widow; whatever larger meaning the event had for her, being alone and raising the surviving children, including one with whom she was pregnant, loomed paramount.

For those who had been leaders in the Church, the deaths meant finding a successor. As long as Joseph was there, the exact question of succession could be left ambiguous. If the Church was to survive in the face of increasing threats and violence, someone had to stand at the head and make decisions. The options and the process of that emergent leadership are subjects dealt with elsewhere, but we can say that in practical terms it was the Twelve, with Brigham Young as president, who took the reins of leadership.

For all Church members, from the Smith family members to new converts, from those in the inner social circles of Nauvoo to members in Tennessee and England, the feeling of grief and loss was quickly combined with the word "martyr." Joseph's and Hyrum's were not just ordinary deaths; they did not simply parallel the deaths of prominent political leaders. They had died for their faith and had sealed their testimony with their blood, and therefore their murder could properly be described as a martyrdom.

The concept of martyrdom had, of course, been part of Christian experience since the martyrdom of Stephen as recorded in the Acts of the Apostles. W. H. C. Frend's authoritative study *Martyrdom and Persecution in the Early Church* (1965) points out how the idea was taken over by persecuted Christians in the second century. They were witnesses and their death for their faith gave added force to their testimony. They were "sealed" by death. Significantly, they saw their death as an imitation of Christ's death, and they were thought to be taken immediately to heaven or Paradise, out of reach of their enemies, there to plan and work with the Lord for the coming of the millennium. The early Christians drew these ideas not only from the Gospel of John, Acts, and the epistles, but also from Maccabean literature, the Maccabees being regarded as the "prototypes of martyrdom" and "prefigurations of Christian martyrdom." Drawing from biblical passages, early Christians found ample assurance that persecution even unto death was simply evidence that they were God's chosen people.

It should not be surprising that Mormons tapped these concepts, for they saw themselves as the modern representatives of God's true church on earth. As soon as there was any kind of opposition or harassment, it was quickly viewed as persecution. As soon as there were actual deaths, the victims were praised as "martyrs." I am tempted to see John Foxe's *Book of the Martyrs* as the widely available account that provided the terminology for the Saints, but in point of fact the conceptualization was built into the situation. Every Christian group that has been outside the mainstream, especially the radical Protestants of the sixteenth century, has seen its experience in terms of persecution and the suffering of martyrdom. During the 1830s the Mormons took over this phraseology, finding it especially comforting during the Missouri persecutions. In 1839 Joseph Smith, then safe in Illinois, wrote of those Mormons who had lost their lives: "And although some of our beloved brethren have had to seal their testimony with their blood, and have died martyrs to the cause of truth—Short though bitter was their pain, / Everlasting is their joy."[1]

So the paradigm by which Joseph Smith's death would be

explained and rationalized was already present in the minds of Mormons. God's people have always been persecuted; martyrs are the highest kind of Saints who pay the ultimate price; they seal their testimony with their blood; they then pass beyond the power of their enemies, and God's cause on earth continues and will still ultimately triumph. These ideas were readily applied to the deaths of the Prophet and Patriarch. The elements were already floating in the atmosphere from which the surviving Saints would construct their comforting explanation after the tragic deaths in June of 1844. Like all martyrs, the dead Prophet and Patriarch had been innocent victims. Their blood was the confirming seal on their life's mission. "The blood of the martyrs is the seed of the church," said an old Christian maxim. Not surprisingly, C. C. A. Christensen used this very expression as the caption for his dramatic, primitivist painting of the assassination scene.[2]

In earlier chapters we reviewed some of the prose and poetry by which the Latter-day Saints, confronted with the unwelcome but inescapable reality of their Prophet's abrupt departure, sought catharsis and meaning. One of the most effective statements—and the only one canonized by inclusion in the LDS Doctrine and Covenants—was penned by eyewitness John Taylor:

> Joseph Smith, the Prophet and Seer of the Lord, has done more, save Jesus only, for the salvation of men in this world, than any other man that ever lived in it. In the short space of twenty years, he has brought forth the Book of Mormon, which he translated by the gift and power of God, and has been the means of publishing it on two continents; has sent the fulness of the everlasting gospel, which it contained, to the four quarters of the earth; has brought forth the revelations and commandments which compose this book

of Doctrine and Covenants, and many other wise documents and instructions for the benefit of the children of men; gathered many thousands of the Latter-day Saints, founded a great city, and left a fame and name that cannot be slain. He lived great, and he died great in the eyes of God and his people; and like most of the Lord's anointed in ancient times, has sealed his mission and his works with his own blood; and so has his brother Hyrum. In life they were not divided, and in death they were not separated!

These are the same ideas that were expressed in diaries, letters, and poetry, but here they come across with the voice of official pronouncement.

In the years following, the martyrdom was not forgotten. Even though the Mormons preferred to emphasize Smith's life and positive contributions, his death, as they saw it, was an essential part of the story—the final demonstration of his veracity and absolute commitment to his prophetic mission. As we have seen, from time to time poets, writers, and artists would look back to the day of his death.

In remembering Joseph Smith's life, however, the martyrdom was but one brief moment and that not the most important. It never became the occasion for a macabre ceremony or reenactment. Here, as in their overall understanding, the Saints were careful to distinguish the violent death of their leader from the far greater atonement and crucifixion of the Lord Jesus Christ.

The fact remains, though, that Joseph Smith with his brother Hyrum suffered a violent death. What if they had said something like, "The jig is up. We admit it, we're frauds. We'll cooperate. We'll give up our scam. Sorry about that, everybody." Can we doubt that they might have saved their lives? But they did not reverse direction and abandon that which had given meaning to their lives. They longed for their families, comforted one another, sang about Jesus, and read about meeting before the judgment bar.

The Latter-day Saints have not forgotten. Intermittently, mention will be made of the martyrdom in conference addresses, in *Church News* articles and editorials, in lessons or talks in the wards throughout the Church. And of course any study of the life of Joseph Smith or the history of the Church must include the emotional events at Carthage. In these different ways the memory of the martyrdom is perpetuated.

I have learned that it is possible if we listen very carefully to hear words that are not part of the historical record. Whether this is the right hemisphere of the brain clammering for attention or what used to be called the heart, I do not know. In any case, true to everything we do know about his attitude, I seem to hear Joseph Smith speaking across time:

"My dear friends, I was not perfect. Like you, I was on the path. It is called the strait and narrow path. I suffered physically in my own life, suffered even more for the persecution endured by the Saints. I had to have some release, and in my lighter moments may not have always been properly serious. I am sorry if some were scandalized by this. On those matters basic to the mission the Lord called me to— on those I think I did not fail. I know this was my constant prayer.

"That last night in Carthage Jail, I took some comfort in reading a passage from the book of Ether. It included words like *charity* (I hope you can feel charity towards each other and towards me) and *faithful* (I hope I was faithful to my mission) and *weakness* (heaven knows I had my share of weaknesses but constantly prayed that these could become strong unto me). The ancient prophet spoke of saying *farewell* and of meeting before the judgment seat of Christ. Somehow, that night in the jail, these words seemed appropriate. I think maybe my brethren, those closest to me, understood them in 1844. Do they communicate with anyone in the 1990s? Farewell."

Yes, brother Joseph, we hear. One only was perfect—Jesus Christ. When you speak of mistakes, we can understand. The Lord will judge you and he will judge us. You lived only a short life. How they must have flown, those thirty-eight years and six months! Yet what an incredible amount you accomplished! Not in the tawdry things of the world but in matters that reach across the years to eternity. By your prophetic deeds our lives have been inestimably deepened and ennobled. Yes, brother Joseph, we hear, we hear.

NOTES

1. Joseph Smith, *History of the Church of Jesus Christ of Latter-day Saints* (Salt Lake City: Deseret News, 1932) 3:330.
2. The C. C. A. Christensen painting, the original of which is at Brigham Young University, is reproduced in *Art in America* (May–June 1970). See also *Ensign* (December 1979).

APPENDIX

TWO MINUTES IN JAIL
by Willard Richards

Possibly the following events occupied near three minutes, but I think only about two, and have penned them for the gratification of many friends.

Carthage, June 27th 1844

A shower of musket balls were thrown up the stairway against the door of the prison in the second story, followed by many rapid footsteps. While Generals Joseph and Hyrum Smith, Mr. Taylor, and myself, who were in the front chamber, closed the door of our room, against the entry at the head of the stairs, and placed ourselves against it, there being no lock on the door and no ketch that was useable. The door is a common panel, and as soon as we heard the feet at the stairs head, a ball was sent through the door, which passed between us, and showed that our enemies were desperadoes, and we must change our position. Gen. Joseph Smith, Mr. Taylor, and myself sprang back to the front part of the room, and Gen. Hyrum Smith retreated two-thirds across the chamber directly in front of and facing the door. A ball was sent through the door which hit Hyrum on the side of his nose when he fell backwards extended at length without moving his feet. From the holes in his vest, (the day was warm and no one had their coats on but myself,) pantaloons, drawers and shirt, it appears evident that a ball must have been thrown from without, through the window, which entered his back on the right side and passing through lodged against his watch which was in his right vest pocket completely pulverizing the crystal and face, tearing off the hands and mashing the whole body of the watch, at the same instant the ball from the door entered his nose. As he struck the floor he exclaimed emphatically; *"I'm a dead man."* Joseph looked towards him, and responded, "O dear *Brother Hyrum,*" and opening the door two or three inches with his left hand, discharged one barrel of a six shooter (Pistol) at random in the entry from whence a ball grazed Hyrum's breast, and entering his throat, passed into his head, while other muskets were aimed at him, and some balls hit him. Joseph continued snapping his revolver, round the casing of the door into the space as before, three barrels of which missed fire, while Mr. Taylor with a walking stick stood by his side and knocked down the bayonets and muskets, which were constantly discharging through the door way, while I stood by him, ready to lend assistance, with another stick, but could not come within striking distance, without going directly before the muzzle of the guns. When the revolver failed, we had no more fire arms, and expecting an immediate rush of the mob, and the door way full of muskets—half way in the room, and no hope but instant death from within: Mr. Taylor rushed into the window, which is some fifteen or twenty feet from the ground. When his body was nearly on a balance, a ball from the door within entered his leg, and a ball from without struck his watch, a patent lever, in his vest pocket, near the left breast, and smashed it in "pie," leaving the hands standing 5 o'clock, 16 minutes, and 26 seconds,—the force of which ball threw him back on the floor, and he rolled under the bed which stood by his side, where he lay motionless, the mob from the door continuing to fire upon him, cutting away a piece of flesh from his left hip as large as a man's hand, and were hindered only by my knocking down their muzzles with a stick; while they continued to reach their guns into the room, probably left handed, and aimed their discharge so far around as almost to reach us in the corner of the room to where we retreated and dodged, and then I recommenced the attack with my stick again. Joseph attempted as the last resort, to leap the same window from whence Mr. Taylor fell, when two balls pierced him from the door, and one entered his right breast from without, and he fell outward exclaiming, "*O Lord my God!*" As his feet went out of the window my head went in, the balls whistling all around. He fell on his left side a dead man. At this instant the cry was raised, "*He's leaped the window,*" and the mob on the stairs and in the entry ran out. I withdrew from the window, thinking it of no use to leap out on a hundred bayonets, then around Gen. Smith's body. Not satisfied with this I again reached my head out of the window and watched some seconds, to see if there were any signs of life, regardless of my own, determined to see the end of him I loved; being fully satisfied, that he was dead, with a hundred men near the body and more coming round the corner of the jail, and expecting a return to our room I rushed towards the prison door, at the head of the stairs, and through the entry from whence the firing had proceeded, to learn if the doors into the prison were open. When near the entry, Mr. Taylor called out "*take me;*" I pressed my way till I found all doors unbarred, returning instantly caught Mr. Taylor under my arm, and rushed by the stairs into the dungeon, or inner prison, stretched him on the floor and covered him with a bed in such a manner as not likely to be perceived, expecting an immediate return of the mob. I said to Mr. Taylor, this is a hard case to lay you on the floor, but if your wounds are not fatal I want you to live to tell the story. I expected to be shot the next moment, and stood before the door awaiting the onset.

WILLARD RICHARDS
—*Nauvoo Neighbor,* 24 July 1844

SELECTIVE BIBLIOGRAPHY

Blake, Reed. *24 Hours to Martyrdom.* Salt Lake City: Bookcraft, 1973.

Ellsworth, Paul D. "Mobocracy and the Rule of Law: American Press Reaction to the Murder of Joseph Smith." *Brigham Young University Studies* 28,1 (1979): 71–82.

Gayler, George R. "Governor Ford and the Death of Joseph and Hyrum Smith." *Journal of the Illinois State Historical Society* 50 (Winter 1957): 391–411.

Godfrey, Kenneth W. "Non-Mormon Views of the Martyrdom: A Look at Some Early Published Accounts." *John Whitmer Historical Association Journal* 17 (1987): 12–20.

Huntress, Keith. "Governor Thomas Ford and the Murderers of Joseph Smith." *Dialogue: A Journal of Mormon Thought* 4 (Summer 1969): 41–52.

Murder of an American Prophet: Events and Prejudice Surrounding the Killings of Joseph and Hyrum Smith; Carthage, Illinois, June 27, 1844. San Francisco: Chandler Publishing Co., 1968.

Jessee, Dean C. "Return to Carthage: Writing the History of Joseph Smith's Martyrdom." *Journal of Mormon History* 8 (1981): 3–19.

Jolley, Clifton Holt. "The Martyrdom of Joseph Smith: An Archetypal Study." *Utah Historical Quarterly* 44 (Fall 1976): 329–50.

Lundwall, N. B., ed. *The Fate of the Persecutors of the Prophet Joseph Smith.* Salt Lake City: Bookcraft, 1952.

Oaks, Dallin H., and Marvin S. Hill. *Carthage Conspiracy: The Trial of the Accused Assassins of Joseph Smith.* Urbana: University of Illinois Press, 1975.

Porter, Larry C. "How Did the U.S. Press React When Joseph and Hyrum Were Murdered?" *Ensign* 14 (April 1984): 22–23.

Poulson, Richard C. "Fate of the Persecutors of Joseph Smith: Transmutation of an American Myth." *Dialogue: A Journal of Mormon Thought* 11, 4 (Winter 1978): 63–70.

Smith, Henry A. *The Day They Murdered the Prophet.* Salt Lake City: Bookcraft, 1963.

INDEX